About the Author

Photograph: Martin Barrow

Born in 1969, Sarah is a mother to two children and three rescue dogs. She is a creative force and a lover of nature. Coping with the rollercoaster that is bipolar affective disorder, Sarah has found strength in writing and, more recently, veganism. As with everything, Sarah wants to share her new-found focus with others.

SARAH J. JAY

ROOTED

The Hiccups & Hurrahs of
Becoming a Vegan Family

With photographs by the author

Copyright © Sarah J. Jay (2016)

The right of Sarah J. Jay to be identified as author of this work has been asserted by her in accordance with section 77 and 78 of the Copyright, Designs and Patents Act 1988.

All rights reserved. No part of this publication may be reproduced, stored in a retrieval system, or transmitted in any form or by any means, electronic, mechanical, photocopying, recording, or otherwise, without the prior permission of the publishers.

Any person who commits any unauthorized act in relation to this publication may be liable to criminal prosecution and civil claims for damages.

A CIP catalogue record for this title is available from the British Library.

ISBN: 978-1-78629-213-1 (paperback)
ISBN: 978-1-78629-214-8 (hardback)
ISBN: 978-1-78629-215-5 (eBook)

www.austinmacauley.com

First Published (2016)

Austin Macauley Publishers Ltd.
25 Canada Square
Canary Wharf
London
E14 5LQ

The first animal-free cookbook, *Kitchen Philosophy for Vegetarians*, was published in England in 1849 by William Horsell of London.

William Horsell

A review of the book claimed that '…butter and eggs are excluded' (*Vegetarian Advocate*, September 1849, p10), making it the first known 'Vegan' cookbook.

'The soul is the same in all living creatures, although the body of each is different.'

Hippocrates 460-370BC, father of Western medicine.

Dedication

This book is dedicated to my partner, Sean, who has supported my journey thus far and accompanied me in vegan eating as well as encouraging the writing of this book. It is also dedicated to all those who fight for the rights of *all* earthlings, and to the animals who have suffered because of the part I played in their exploitation, before I questioned my doubts and became a vegan.

With love to my son Jack & daughter Emily & to my Mum, Jenny, forever.

The biggest dedication of all goes to HARPO, our much loved and so missed miniature English Bull Terrier. He taught us what it means to be loyal, loving, patient and humble. He made me think again about my attitude toward all animals. He made me a better human being. He was a champ. We love him still. Bless you Harpo.

Acknowledgements

With many thanks to Kevin Twomey (great friend and advisor), Kathryn, Hugo, Arthur & Charlie Bragg (food tasters), Margaret & Ernest Easterby (tasters & crockery givers), and all those on my Facebook pages (Fearless Vegan Food Blog, Fearless Vegan Recipes) who have been supportive of all my efforts at each and every step.

The avatar I use for my Facebook page!

Contents

Welcome to *Rooted* 13
    An Introduction – A Good Start 15
    Before you start… 19
    Equipment 20
    The Five Absolute Must-Haves in the Larder 23
    The 'Hiccups' Scrapbook! 25
    Skill Set 28
        Making Nut Milk (and single cream) 28
        Making Pastry 29
        A Word about Cooking Curry 33
        Cooking Vegan Sponge Cake 34
        Preparing Oaties for the Oven 36
        Pressing Tofu 38
        Straining Yoghurt 39
        The Tin Glossary 40
        Lentils: A Vegan Staple? 43
        Mushrooms: Friend or Foe? 44
    Oven Temperature Conversion 46
    English Across the Pond 47

RECIPES
(The 'Hurrahs!') 49

Soup, Stock & Bread 51
    Traditional Casseroled Vegetable Stock 52
    Stove-top Aromatic Vegetable Stock 53
    Aromatic Vegetable Soup 54
    Moroccan Style Lentil Soup 55
    Aromatic Curried Lentil Soup 57
    Cream of Celeriac Soup 58
    Cream of Tomato Soup 59
    Sun-Dried Tomato Tea Soup 61
    Pea & Roasted Parsnip Soup 63
    All Season Soup 64
    Focaccia (Italian Bread) 65
    Basic Flat Bread 67
    Naan Inspired Flat Bread 68
    Multi Seed Bloomer 69
    Sun-Dried Tomato & Pumpkin Seed Bread 70

Paté, Spreads & Sauces ... 71

- Rich Tomato, Pepper & Mushroom Sauce ... 72
- Sweet Chilli Red Wine Sauce ... 74
- Roast Potatoes ... 75
- Gravy ... 76
- Sweet Chestnut Paté ... 79
- Fig & Chestnut Paté ... 80
- Pecan, Apple & Red Wine Paté (Baked) ... 83
- Almond, Chestnut & Red Wine Paté ... 84
- Smoked Toasted Almond & Chilli Paté (Baked) ... 85
- Paté Nuggets ... 86
- Hummus ... 88
- Chilli & Turmeric Hummus ... 89
- Mayonnaise ... 90
- Coleslaw ... 91
- Potato Salad ... 92
- Cucumber, Mint & Lemon Raita ... 94
- 'Cheesy' Cream Sauce ... 95
- Basil Cream Pasta Sauce ... 96
- Pasta Salad ... 97
- Sarah's Bombay Potatoes ... 98
- Grilled Courgettes ... 99
- Smoked Paprika Chips ... 101
- Onion Side Salad ... 103
- Stir-Fry Sauces ... 104
- Main Salads ... 106
- Dressings ... 108

Main Dishes... 109

- Classic Ratatouille ... 111
- Chilli ... 112
- Gentle Fusion Dal ... 113
- Button Mushrooms in Sweet Chestnut Sauce ... 114
- Baked Bean & New Potato Pie ... 116
- Sticky Fruit 'n' Nut Curried Rice ... 118
- Mediterranean Stew & Herb Dumplings ... 120
- Three Bean Curry ... 122
- Sweet Chilli Vegetables ... 124
- Cottage Pie ... 125
- Rich Nut Loaf ... 128

- Coconut & Lime Curry ... 131
- Red Rice & Polenta Burgers ... 135
- Classic Chilli Bean Burger ... 136
- Cajun & Ginger Burgers ... 138
- Garam Masala Lentil Stew ... 139
- Mushroom & Broccoli Pie ... 141
- Stew & Dumplings ... 144
- Lasagne ... 147
- Stir-Fry Vegetables with Toasted Peanuts ... 149
- Winter Vegetable Pie ... 150

Sweet Delights ... 153
- Fruit Smoothies ... 155
- Fruit Salad ... 157
- Coconut Rice Pudding ... 159
- Roasted Hazelnut & Chocolate Chunk Cookies ... 160
- Spiced Basmati Rice Pudding ... 161
- Pineapple & Rum Upside-Down Cake ... 162
- Strawberries & Cream Tart ... 164
- Coconut, Orange & Raspberry Cake ... 166
- Double Chocolate & Pecan 'Brownie' Biscuits ... 168
- Chocolate & Cashew Butter Mousse ... 171
- Raspberry Frangipane ... 172
- Citrus 'Cheesecake' ... 174
- Spiced Fruit Tea Loaf ... 177
- Lemon Sponge Tray Bake ... 179
- Peanut Butter & Banana Oatie ... 183
- Almond & Coconut Biscuits ... 185
- Cashew & Coffee Mousse ... 186
- Raspberry Syllabub ... 189
- Celebration / Christmas Cake ... 190
- Carrot Cake Tray Bake ... 193
- Rum & Chocolate Tart ... 195
- Peanut Butter Oatie ... 198
- Crispy Nut & Orange Oatie ... 199
- Cherry Brandy Chocolate Whip ... 200
- Moist Fruit Cake ... 203
- Jam Roly Poly ... 204
- Sweet 'n' Salt Peanut Butter Whip ... 206
- Tropical Yoghurt Tart ... 209

 Plum & Elderflower Crumble 211
 Moist Chocolate Sponge Tray Bake 212
 Coffee Sponge Cake with Chocolate Butter Cream 215
 Dessert Sauces 217
One Meal into Many 218
The Talkie Bit 221
 How did **Rooted** happen? 222
 My Own Reasons for Being a Vegan 226
 First Errors 228
 Make a List 232
 Foraging in the Aisles 234
 Home with the Groceries 239
 Integrity of Ingredients 241
 Knowing & Sticking with your Onions 245
 Veganism and Direct Action 250
 Making it Easier on You 251
 Eating Out 254
 A Life-Long Purity 257
 The Protein & Cholesterol Confusion 260
 Where Now 263
 Useful References 266

WELCOME TO
ROOTED

'It is important to say that everything in this book is my own viewpoint and my own experience, and none of it represents the interests of any other party, association, group or individual. This book does not set out to explain veganism or to convert anyone to it. I hope only that it offers ideas, comfort and confidence to readers looking for a book to accompany their own vegan journey, their own transition from an omnivorous life to a vegan one.'

Sarah Jay, July 2015

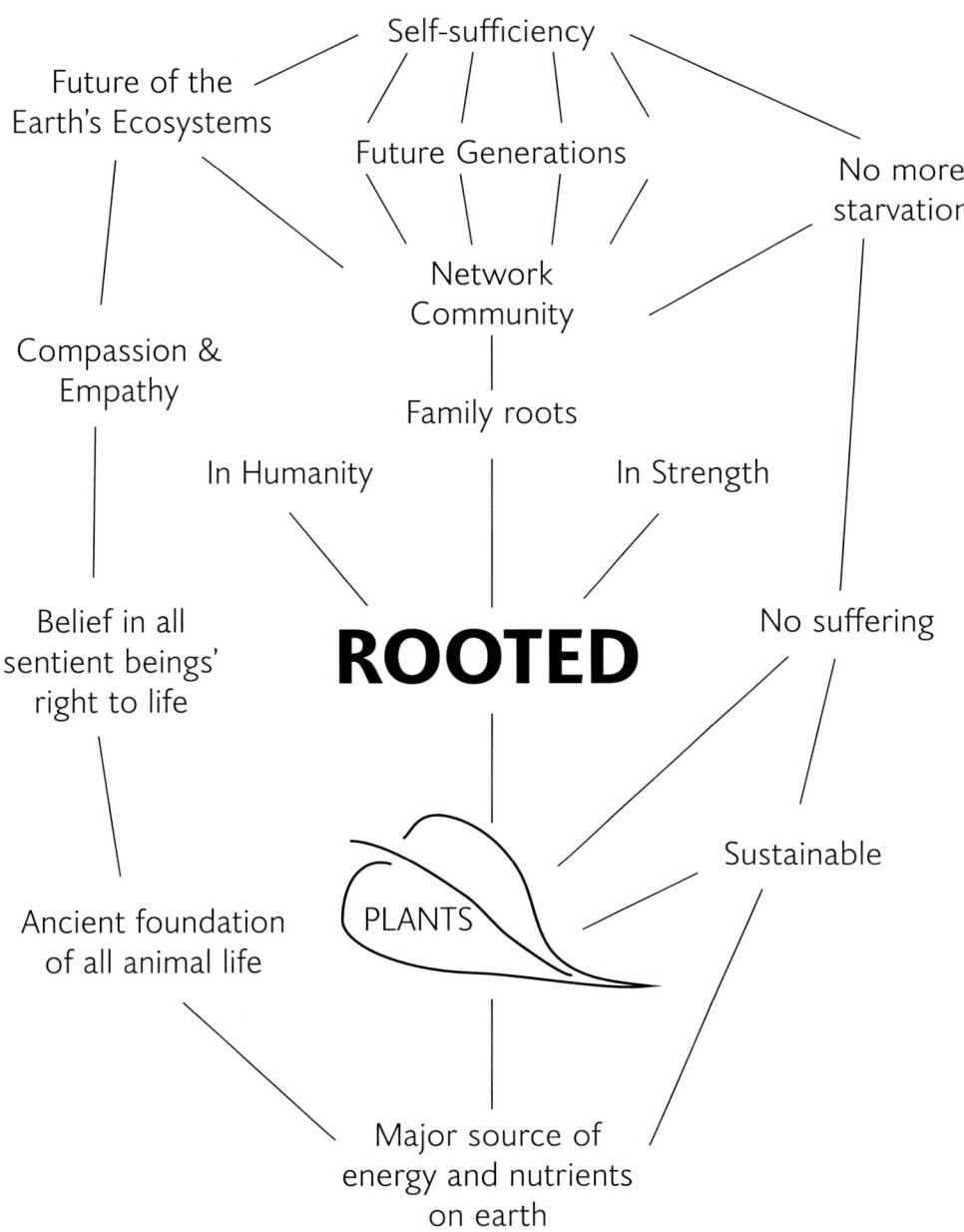

The many meanings of 'Rooted'

An Introduction – A Good Start

My family and I transitioned to a vegan life two years ago, and to say it was easy would be putting a gloss over the truth, and mislead others looking for honest help, support and ideas. But we have not regretted our journey thus far. Quite the opposite. I wish we had done this many years ago.

This book is in response to my experiences as cook with a grown family and to those I have talked with who have seemed in need of a guide that was, until now, unavailable. We shared this need to be helped at that first stage in transition from omnivore to vegan and to give those of us who are not particularly health-conscious a chance to keep our best loved foods in our lives. Vegan does not necessarily mean healthy, but in its simplest terms just means animal-free. Too many vegans and vegan-oriented places seem to push the healthy option too readily, and forget those of us who have a sweet and sometimes gorging tooth, who will not let go of the pie and mash and gateaux quite so readily.

Rooted does not try to convert anyone. It assumes that if a person has picked this book up, then they either know me from my Facebook or Twitter blogs (see 'Useful References; My Contacts', page 266), are vegan or vegetarian, or already making their way towards a decision to become one or the other. It does however try to explain, in part, how we in this country have continued eating omnivorously for so long, even though we like to think of ourselves as a nation of animal-lovers. It does not shy away from some of the ethical issues, but also accepts that not everyone comes to veganism from an ethical standpoint. It can be for many reasons and that is the reader's business. **I do not judge, only encourage the perseverance sometimes required to remain vegan.**

My own children may be grown up, but I keep in mind the family with young children and older relatives as I write these pages, and hope the vegan door is opened for you as a family unit. My recipes are designed with this goal in mind for you. This book is further supported by my Facebook pages offering other free recipes and information, particularly *Fearless Vegan Food Blog* and *Fearless Vegan Recipes*.

Before I begin to share some of my own chequered attempts at transition to veganism, just one piece of advice I would like to give, that I would like you to keep uppermost in your mind.

Vegans eat food just like everyone else. It is the decisions about ingredients that define a vegan diet. Much of what you already eat (if you are an omnivore) is already vegan, but you just haven't thought *of it that way before. Therefore there is already much in your kitchen that you will be able to use as ingredients. You are not beginning your journey with an empty set of kitchen cupboards.*

Admittedly, I began my journey ill-informed and ill-read with regard to diet, and the little I had read made me feel less than motivated. Books and online 'help', often written by competent and well-meaning vegan cooks, seemed to concentrate on the *successes* in the kitchen. I felt a little bit unworthy, as they seemed never to speak of being tempted outside the vegan life, of making mistakes, on how to control the urge to eat what is not vegan or about the frustrating failures in their kitchens as they experimented with new ingredients. Nor did they give advice about coping with being known as 'a vegan' by all of those around you and on social networking sites.

As a member of many vegan online groups (see 'Useful References', page 266), it was obvious that vegans were often using these platforms to find people with similar experiences and difficulties to share advice on how to deal with the challenges and temptations faced by vegans. This included dealing with other people's prejudices, often – surprisingly – from family and close friends. It seemed that the very label 'vegan' carried with it negative misconceptions. Perhaps that is why I am not as comfortable with the word 'vegan' as I should be, and prefer to say I follow a plant-based or 'rooted' diet, hence the title of this book. Misconceptions will be looked at in more detail later.

Help was out there in various forms in various places, but there didn't seem to be a book that I could hold and read and go to that had the motivational advice I needed, wrapped up with solid, tempting and practical cooking ideas. Many of the publications I looked at were published in the US and these have challenges of their own. Different vocabulary and measuring units, and foods that are hard to source in the UK, all make following a US recipe book rather tricky. The last thing you want when transitioning from omnivore to vegan is a book that you need to make allowances for. I try here to include US measures as I find cups and spoon measures very useful. I would suggest you think of purchasing these little tools yourself.

It seemed to me that vegan cooking, the vegan embrace of lifestyle, and maintaining that life against a tide of misunderstanding and prejudice from the most surprising of corners, were being approached as separate topics, dealt with in very different arenas, when actually all aspects of veganism were interconnected in such a way as to be, in my humble opinion, indistinguishable, particularly in the case of 'newbie' vegans.

The early days saw me less than excited by the six different vegan recipe books I initially purchased (I really had no idea about finding information online at this time). All were pretty cheap so they had little or no pictures, and very concise instructions. Some had pages and pages of nutritional information which I found very off-putting, and seemed to invest the reader with a fear that becoming vegan meant the danger of malnutrition, unless you took up nutritional science as a hobby. Such information is rarely included in such mammoth detail in omnivorous cook books. There seemed to be ingredients I had never heard of and certainly couldn't get hold of in my own town. Food was being treated and plated as if it came from another planet, and that had to be off-putting to many – it certainly was to me.

Something else struck me early on. A lot of vegan writers and bloggers are young health enthusiasts, often without children, or people who have had health scares and turned vegan to save their lives and future health. Either way, they are motivated by a drive towards optimum health. I too want to be healthy and provide healthy food for my family, but not to the point these people take it; to be fair, I felt it was not representative of most of the society. I didn't know a single person who actually ate a raw diet, ran five miles a day and did yoga before breakfast and gym at night. Such a lifestyle would probably kill me although there are those who swear by such disciplined health regimes. I felt this needed addressing. *Veganism is not about super-health, or optimum health. It is about not eating animal derived products (along with many other aspects). It is up to the individual how healthy they make their vegan diets.*

Having been a mother for twenty-plus years, and a good omnivorous cook, I had a sure and solid set of meals, puddings, treats and celebration menus that worked for me and my family. After my Nan got too old to manage, I took over providing the Christmas Dinner for the family, the birthday teas and any other gathering that required food. If I was to change the very foundation of what we ate, I was going to have to be really sure that I and my family were going to be happy and well-fed and motivated to stay that way.

I admit it is scary knowing that, as the cook, you will be leaving behind years of skill and trying things that are new, but many of your current skills are transferable. Most of us are not trained; we have learnt through experience and advice passed down the generations, our grandmothers, aunts and of course, mothers. But most of us don't have that support when it comes to vegan cooking. I want that to change.

Surely there were others out there like me, who were put off contemplating making the change towards vegan food because it just didn't look familiar and they simply didn't frequent online food blogs or vegan groups where they might find what they were looking for. What is more, their children, who may be fussy eaters, and the older generation of the family who liked things as they had always been, may all be pretty set *against* change. Let's face it, for the uninformed majority, vegans were pasty, skinny individuals who still wore sandals, headbands and broke wind far more than most due to the mushy lentil and pulse diet. (I have to admit to the latter, but I was the same on an omnivorous diet!) And most people cannot seem to see why eating animal products should be any kind of issue in the first place.

As an omnivore one of my favourite dishes was sausages with onions and gravy. Like many (slightly panicky) transitioning vegans I tried to replace my favourites with 'copycat' vegan alternatives, trying every type of vegan sausage I could find. They all disappointed me, so much so that I simply stopped trying to replace the old with imitation new. For me it didn't work. Instead, I simply accepted that as a vegan I wouldn't be eating sausages any more – a small sacrifice to pay for doing the right thing, in my view. What that attitude did, was drive me to make brand new alternatives that satisfied in place of the old favourites. What surprised me was how much better my own creations were.

At this point I would like to stress that there are many ready-made foods, including vegan sausages, that are available in the UK and abroad, but where I live, there just isn't anywhere I know of. So I took that as a challenge to be faced full-on, and so began this recipe collection.

As the weeks rolled by, I craved food that I used to eat, the flavours of roast dinner, pie and gravy, jam roly-poly and trifle, the very food that was part of my childhood. I needed to create food that I loved, and I wanted to share that food. There is nothing better in life than helping others. To do that I needed a platform and a style of address that grabbed people's attention **then held it continually day after day.** Whether a person visited the platform for health reasons or for ethical, *it had to hold hope and deliciousness, to reflect something British and something that had been handed down the generations.* And it had to be exciting or I felt I would lose momentum and starve, along with my family who were relying on me to feed them this new-fangled food – and then teach them how to cook it for themselves!

This book is the consolidation of the first two years of my goal to share, to accompany those who are, like me, transitioning but wanting familiar, family foods. It is a beginning, but one that provides what I hope is a firm foundation for you to build upon, that keeps you and yours vegan for the rest of your life.

Before you start...

Everyday home cooking is a craft. It is not a gift as some might like to think, nor is it a knack. It takes practice, patience and method. Even when you don't follow a recipe, you still need to be organised to be able to enjoy the experience, and that is my top tip. There is nothing worse than being part way through cooking and realising you need two tablespoons of tomato purée, only to find that it has run out, or measuring it out takes just enough time for your curry to burn!

- Like making a journey, plan out what you need, including equipment as well as ingredients. Be prepped before you cook, and keep notes of new or altered recipes. Then creativity is free to really make its mark.

- Read through the recipe and just check you have what is needed. Then measure out as much as you can in readiness. This is essential for things like stir-fries and curries where the actual cooking is very fast but involves a lot of different ingredients. But it is a good habit to get into, especially if you are a novice to cooking.

- Prep things like baking/roasting tins before you start cooking. Set up whisks, processors or blenders beforehand, making sure **they are clean and all the attachments are near at hand. Get** out the bits and bobs you need, so you won't have to open drawers and cupboards with sticky or floury hands.

- Wipe down surfaces you will use before cooking. When making bread or pastry I actually use a waterproof tablecloth as this protects my table from getting scoured by seeds and wholemeal flour, and is easy to wipe clean. It is also great for rolling out pastry.

- If you are making something that requires chilling, **check** you have room in the fridge first and clear an area in the fridge ready. I have been stung by that myself, having finished a big mousse or tart only to find my fridge full of yesterday's newly purchased groceries!

- If you are making large amounts of something make sure you have containers large or numerous enough for storage, and if freezing, that you have freezer space. This may sound obvious but in the rush of inspiration it is the obvious and mundane details that get overlooked.

- Then enjoy it! Good food happens when you love it. Treat the ingredients with respect and enthusiasm. It will then surprise you with taste, colour and texture, and if it goes wrong, there is always that can of beans! Believe me, we have had our fair share of beans on toast over the past six months.

Equipment

As far as equipment goes, you really don't need anything too special. I did get myself a mini food processor, which has been essential, and I suggest this be the one thing you get if you don't already have one. An electric hand blender is better than nothing.

If you like spices and curries and you think you may get into this area of cooking I suggest you get a little electric coffee grinder, for grinding your own spices. It makes a huge difference and whole seeds stay fresh longer than ground spice, so grinding just enough for the dish you are cooking means less waste. Flavour and heat is not lost this way.

Blenders are all the rage since the 'smoothie' came into being, and they can blend just about anything, but they vary in cost and performance. There are commercial blender grinders available for £700 or more, so be careful. Look for the £100-£200 mark as this budget provides the maximum power you will ever need in your own kitchen. Mine is a BERG 1500W, and it copes with anything I throw into or at it. I have never needed to use it on full power – it scares the heck out of me and my dogs! I haven't used it as much as I thought I would, usually opting for my food processor. But I intend to use it more in the future as I explore different ingredients and cooking methods.

- Mini food processor
- Small non-stick frying pan
- Bread tin
- A hand whisk and a rasp or mini grater
- Silicon spatula and a slotted spoon
- Measuring cups
- Hand juicer
- Measuring spoons
- Two spring form tins and a loose bottomed fluted flan tin
- Stockpot or large saucepan with lid

Many items are non-expensive and sold in supermarkets, though that is not always the cheapest stockist. I added a new item each week/month if I could afford it, and scrounged a few others off my partner's mother. Any time someone is doing a clear-out, try to get a new dish or storage container to add to your own equipment. Second-hand shops are great for finding some really lovely useful things and also dishes and bowls for serving. Watch out for the sales and end-of-line shelves in supermarkets or home stores. I think serving things in an attractive way when you have visitors, or just feeding the family around the table really helps get them to try new foods. We rely so much on how things look. Make that work to your advantage.

NOTES

The Five Absolute Must-Haves in the Larder

There is a section on what to buy for your kitchen cupboards and fridge in the 'Talkie Bit' at the end of the book (page 234). Here I would like to emphasise how crucial these particular five items are, and why. They are the sort of thing you might not have or have even heard of before, and I don't want that to put you off in any way. I really can't understand why omnivores don't use these things too, because they are so useful. Yet I know that I myself had never heard of item number 2 or 3 until I became a vegan. You will find it frustrating to follow the recipes in this book without these items.

1) SOYA – in the form of firm silken tofu, milk, butter (margarine), cream and flour

I don't like the taste of soya and it is argued by some that one should not use it in excess of other bean and nut sources, yet it is enormously useful and does provide protein. I use it in this book in various ways, including making staples such as mayonnaise, sauces, pastry, sponges and a whole list of things that require a little of it to give moisture or smoothness, like cream in a paté for instance.

One great advantage about soya is that it is now available everywhere so most supermarkets stock it in the various forms, apart from the flour. I only use the flour in the Rich Nut Loaf (page 128), so it really isn't essential. The Tofu is found in Tetra Pak cartons and is not chilled. It keeps for ages too if left unopened.

2) ENER-G EGG REPLACER (UK distributor General Dietary Ltd, available online from various stockists)

What I love about this stuff is it lasts and lasts and never seems to go off! It is a fine white powder, and each box provides the equivalent of around 100 eggs. It works in most of the things I cook, although I am still trying to work out a decent Yorkshire pudding and am wondering if this is really not the right egg substitute.

It is available online and I tend to buy a few boxes which last me about two years! It is cheap and essential. And easy to use. When whisked up with water, milk or juice it forms a convincing albumin-like froth. It can even be used to make meringues!

You will need measuring spoons for it, though, as it is very specific and works best when measured out correctly.

3) NUTRITIONAL YEAST (I use Mari-Gold Engevita Yeast Flakes from online stockists)

This is probably the one thing you haven't heard of. But it is crazy really because this is something we should use for our kids, pregnant women and the elderly instead of buying those vitamin tablets from chemists that cost a small fortune. This is natural, cheap, and easy to use.

It has a very mild cheesy flavour which can be used in savoury sauces, but can be just as easily hidden in stews, soups and mashed potato. Adding it to food instantly adds nutritional value. At only 17 calories per 100g, it provides virtually all your daily needs of the B Vitamin family (Thiamine B1, Riboflavin B2, Niacin B3, B6, B12), Folic Acid and Zinc. Make sure you buy one fortified with extra Vitamin B12.

4) MARMITE & SUN-DRIED TOMATOES

I have classed these as one thing because they get used for the same thing in my cooking and neither one could I eat alone. Marmite is a love-it-or-hate-it sort of food, but that doesn't matter in this case, because it is used rather like a beef stock cube. Let's face it, you wouldn't eat a stock cube, would you, but you still use them to flavour things. That is what I use Marmite for (and Vegemite can also be used), in very small amounts to gravies and sauces mostly. Sun-dried tomatoes are amazing. The ones in oil are the best since they really do bring with them a rich, fleshy flavour that makes things 'meaty'. I use them all the time.

5) READY COOKED SWEET CHESTNUTS

Chestnuts are usually with the stuffing mixes in supermarkets. They go into patés and into gravy – in fact they are the base of gravy for me. You don't taste them much at all (although they bring a sweet mild flavour which is nice), but they provide a substance and colour to the gravy, to which all the other flavourings are added. Not to mention they are packed with protein, vitamins and minerals too. They are a super-food in my opinion.

That is why they are so easy to use as nuts sliced in stir-fry and in rice dishes, but be warned: their texture is a little pasty, and not to my own liking. That is why they are so easy to blitz into a paste for gravy and sauce bases. Apparently they are heavenly with chocolate and I have begun to use them in desserts…

The 'Hiccups' Scrapbook!

It was important that this book be true to the experience of becoming a vegan cook. So sharing some of the mishaps needs to be done, and here I have compiled a little gallery of food that looked okay, but tasted wrong, or felt wrong or just didn't work! It goes to show that what glitters is not always gold and makes you feel a little better about those celebrity chefs and their immaculate books. Believe me, there would have been failures in their kitchens too. And we don't have years of culinary education and teams of young chefs on hand to do all the chopping, peeling, weighing and washing.

I learnt everything from the mistakes. It was rare that I hit on a success straightaway. You can think of it like a chemistry set: the ingredients in a kitchen can work together in a number of ways but not all of them work as food. If you really don't have much of a clue, and are not using many guides to help you, then realistically there are going to be cooking casualties. Just make sure they don't end up on someone's plate and that you note down what went wrong so you can learn from it.

- A first attempt at a mini mushroom pie. The pastry was good and the pie structure worked, but the filling was salty and didn't taste of mushrooms!
- A coconut and lime curry attempt. Wasn't bad but I hated the chickpea texture and it all looked hideous when photographed. Worked better later.
- Another attempt at that mushroom pie. Better but still salty – I realise now it was the dried mushrooms and the red wine together.
- Orange mousse. Unfortunately not only was it not a mousse but a cream, it also tasted bitter as I had used too much orange zest.
- First use of Agar flakes to set a coconut cream dessert. Tasted like soap! Best bit was the blackberry sauce.
- Made a chocolate tart. Pastry case was perfect but the chocolate filling had too much cornflour in it and could have bounced across the kitchen floor! Based on a book I had, which I decided wasn't for me.
- Based on a recipe in a book, a Chana Dal curry was bland and my Basmati rice was sticky – argh!
- Ruined a perfectly good ratatouille by adding too much cooked quinoa. Weird texture and diluted the flavour. I decided I didn't like quinoa much (although it is highly nutritious).

- Over-roasted vegetables and potatoes. Easily done if you don't keep your eye on the timer!

- First go at chocolate mousse with a cherry syrup – neither thing set! More of a chocolate cream with cherry water!

- Lentil stew with herb vegan dumplings. The dumplings worked but they didn't go with the lentil stew – the two textures together were unpleasant.

- A tofu based dessert that was too wet because I hadn't pressed the tofu enough. Although sloppy it tasted good.

- For my first frangipane attempt (like a Bakewell tart), put on too many fig slices, which sank and made an almond 'slick' rather than a tart.

- Tried a new curry idea which was ruined by too many bell peppers – they made the flavours rather bitter.

- Used Bouillon powder for the first time and ruined a perfectly good vegetable soup. Bouillon too salty for my taste.

I could include around another six pages of this, but I think maybe this sample is enough.

Try not to throw away the written notes you make on a recipe, even if it fails miserably. Build up from them. I kept all my recipes until I had got them right, so I could trace mistakes and make notes about improvements. It wasn't as organised as I am making it sound – just a bunch of bits of paper really, but I now have a little card system with my recipes on. Easy to find and adjust. I admit they are just lists of ingredients. The method gets locked in my head. I do refer now and then to this book myself!

HOW NEW RECIPES BEGIN THEIR JOURNEY

Skill Set

This section is to assist you only if it becomes necessary. Most of the recipes in this book require only basic cooking skills. However, I do use a couple of new skills that I have taught myself and pass on to you now.

Making Nut Milk (and single cream)

This is so much fun, so easy and so much better than bought milk, that I had to include it in this book. This method also makes single cream. I admit I don't make it all the time, but for a treat and to go with fresh warm cookies, I love making a litre or two.

There are two milks I currently make, along with chocolate milk. One requires plain cashews and pecans, and the other requires almonds, blanched or not. If you try this with a small bag of nuts first and find you like it, I recommend you buy further nuts in bulk from a health food supplier. I get mine online. It is far cheaper this way, even when you buy organic.
Whichever nuts you use, the method is exactly the same.

- **Cashew & Pecan** (sweeter than just cashew with a nice pale caramel colour) 1 cup cashews to ½ cup pecans, 2½ -3 cups water plus 6-10 dates to sweeten further and a pinch of salt. Sultanas or figs are good as sweeteners too.

- **Almond** is a more mellow and nutty flavour to the cashew's more buttery finish. Again feel free to mix the nuts up. Use 1½ cups of almonds, 2½–3 cups water, dates, sultanas or figs to taste and pinch of salt.

- **Chocolate Milk** is simply the milks above with raw cacao powder or carob powder added. The amount depends on your taste. I also like some dark brown sugar added which gives a richer flavour, but it isn't quite as health conscious! Add a little ice to add chill and froth. Also add a tablespoon of vegetable oil or margarine to avoid the chalky texture of powdered cacao.

- **Banana Milk** and any other milk is easy to make but the flavouring should be added after the milk has been chilled so its flavour can be better judged. Try banana and chocolate, banana and peach and banana and coconut cream added. Don't forget to add a little ice to help froth it up like a shake.

- **Prune Milk**: I have to add this option because so few people had heard of it when I put it on my Facebook pages, yet it is a hit! Simply use one of your milks – cashew & pecan is preferable, or soya – and add several prunes to it and some ice. Do check for stones as this will ruin the drink! An amazing way to get kids to eat prunes…

Making the Basic Milk:

Firstly, the nuts – any measure you like, but I find 2 cups will make 1¾ Litres of rich milk – need soaking overnight. Place them in a large bowl and cover generously with boiling water. Not only does this soften nuts but it washes out digestion-deterring enzymes which may be present, so making them easier on our gut.

Once soaked, drain off the liquid, rinse once and place into a food processor and chop roughly before adding to the blender with the required water and sweeteners. Blend so that the nuts are completely gone, but not so much that the liquid becomes too smooth. The reason for this will become obvious in a moment.

Now using a muslin square, doubled over, or a clean stocking, pour the liquid in. Do this over a large bowl and carefully close the top of the muslin over and twist and squeeze the muslin bag. The milk will come through, leaving the nut sediment behind. If you over-blend the nuts, fine sediment will get through and you will have a gritty milk. Squeeze until no more liquid will come out. If the milk seems too creamy you can add a little more water to the muslin sediment and squeeze it through.

Chill the milk before drinking or adding fruit or chocolate to it.

Making Pastry

There is no mystery about making a good pastry. The most important points are to treat it with some love rather than fear, and to make sure you don't work it too much. Hot hands and over-manipulating the pastry will make it hard to roll and hard to eat! I only introduce two types of pastry in this book for simplicity and flavour: Short Crust and Vegetable Suet Pastry. Read this section through a couple of times if you are new to pastry making.

Basic Short Crust

Basic Short Crust as used in this book I make my own way. Traditionally the ratio of flour to fat is 2:1 but using non-dairy butter/margarine you will find you need less fat and less water than before. Use the measures I give to start with in the recipes themselves until you feel you can judge the ratios yourself. I stick to soya-based butters as these are less greasy than sunflower- or olive-based ones.

Making Vegan Suet Pastry and Sweet Pie Pastry

Suet pastry simply means that instead of using the non-dairy butter/margarine you replace it with a white vegetable fat which is shredded. It remains in its little bits when added to the flour and rolled as pastry and as it cooks these create a puffed, light and very scrummy pastry, great for pies and Jam Roly Poly. Be generous with salt when making suet pastry.

Sweet pastry is the same as short-crust but an ounce (25-30g) of caster sugar is added and sometimes some lemon zest. Still add a little salt. I also like adding ½ teaspoon of ground mixed spice on occasion.

Remember: I always use soya-based margarine for baking because I find the olive- or sunflower-based ones too 'oily' and they make the pastry very difficult to work with. My measurements are for use with soya-based baking products.

Sometimes if I want the pastry to be more airy or cake-like in texture I use half plain flour and half self-raising flour. An example would be with my fruit pies. You can also make lighter pastry by taking one quarter of the flour away and replacing it with the same weight of cornflour.

Method to Making Pastry

In a mixing bowl place the flour, salt, sugar and fat – whichever is stated in the recipe. Using fingertips, rub the margarine into the flour aiming to coat the flour in the fat, forming a breadcrumb texture. **You do not do this for suet pastry: just stir together.** As you do this, raise your fingers up so you let the flour fall, capturing air between the particles. This makes for lighter pastry.

Now add the water and mix it in using your fingertips, lifting it up in the air again. Once the mixture feels slightly damp, press the mixture together firmly and see if it stays together or falls apart. If it just won't stay together, break it up and add more water, but literally a half a teaspoon at a time. If you add too much too quickly, it will suddenly become wet and adding more flour at this stage will result in hard brittle pastry when cooked.

Once you have pressed the mixture together to form a dough, split it into portions so that you roll out the pie base/s first then have some left for the pie lids. **Don't roll pastry twice if you can help it** – use it once and then bin, or use as decoration only. Once it has been rolled, pressing it back together and re-rolling makes for tough pastry, almost inedible.

When rolling pastry use a floured surface and pin. Roll from the centre up and down once, then swivel the pastry half a turn and roll again and keep going. Don't intentionally roll the very edges of the pastry as these tend to split.

Grease the tin you are going to use with margarine, even if it is non-stick, place and press in your pastry leaving the edges overhanging if making pies, or trimming if making a flan or tart pastry case. Cover with cling film and refrigerate for 30 minutes. This prevents the pastry shrinking when it bakes.

Sometimes you will need to make a ready-cooked pie/tart case without a filling, and when doing this you will need to start by 'baking blind'. Place some foil in first and some baking beans on top (I use raw chickpeas over and over just for this), into the pie base. Bake the pastry on the middle shelf at around 180'C for about 15 minutes, then remove the baking beans and bake another 15-20 minutes.

If you are making a pie with a lid, the pie filling shouldn't be watery. You can 'blind-bake' (that is, bake the pie shell without the filling) for use with runny fillings. However, it becomes difficult to get the pastry bottom to seal with the raw pastry top, so I never blind-bake. I make sure my filling, whether hot savoury or cold sweetened fruit, is not watery and that it contains a thickening agent.

To seal the bottom pastry with the pastry lid, firstly use a pie tin which allows there to be a narrow strip or ledge of pastry free of filling around the circumference, and dampen this with water or non-dairy milk before carefully but confidently lifting the pastry lid on. Make sure you have made it big enough to go over the edges, so you can trim the remainder neatly with a knife after sealing together. Press the two pastry edges together with your thumb and forefinger or handle end of a spoon to seal, and pierce the lid with a fork or knife tip, then bake.

Tip: Even if I am using a non-stick tin I always smear non-dairy margarine on it and sprinkle with flour to form a non-stick boundary between tin and pastry.

Tip: Make sure your hands are cool when you make pastry. It is important to keep ingredients and method as chilled as possible.

Vegan Suet Dumplings

Lots of us have a fear about making dumplings. Such a fear was handed down to me from my grandmother, who made incredible dumplings as it happens, but worried herself silly until they were actually dished up onto the plate. I have no idea why, because they are actually very easy – although I think making them with vegetable suet is far easier and fail-safe than with traditional animal fat, since it is less dense and less liable to sink in a stew.

These dumplings are the British kind: the reasonably plain, slightly salted, fluffy, comforting balls that soak up the gravy and fill the stomach. It seems that every culture has its own kind of dumpling, and once you have made and eaten a batch, you realise why.

Instructions for making these are on the packet of vegetable suet you buy. My tip here is not to under-do the salt. When they steam on top of your stew or soup, keep the lid firmly on for the whole cooking time – do not be tempted to lift it. The pressure of steam built up inside the pan cooks them beautifully. Trust it!

In case you don't have a recipe, just the vegetable suet, then here are the quantities to make eight little dumplings:

- 100g / 4 oz Self Raising Flour
- 50g / 2 oz Vegetable Suet (shredded fat – always keep in fridge as it works better)
- Generous pinch Salt (fine)
- Approx 4-5 tablespoons cold water
- ½ teaspoon mixed dried Herbs (optional)

Place all the dry ingredients together in a bowl and mix. Add the water and then mix with your fingertips. Press it all together to form a firm but pliable dough, which should feel very slightly sticky – this feels very different from pastry. Using floured hands, pull it apart into eight balls of even size and firmly press without compacting, into neat balls. I usually do these before I need to cook them and chill them. They always come up fluffier this way.

To cook, simply place on the top of a simmering soup or stew, place the lid on and leave for 20 minutes. Serve immediately.

Watery soups will not work well as the dumplings need to be at the surface really. If you want to, you could cook the dumplings in a separate pan of simmering vegetable stock with cornflour added to thicken it so the dumplings don't sink completely.

A Word about Cooking Curry

Whenever I tried to make a curry in the past, it never ever had an authentic taste, nor did it have a properly emulsified sauce. I could always feel the powdery ground spices on my tongue.

Knowing that traditional Indian cuisine is largely vegetarian, I decided to purchase a couple of Indian vegan cookbooks to find out about Indian cookery from those that knew it best. I have to admit to not studying it fully, since it is a large and varied area of cooking, but from the ten or so recipes I tried, I picked up some basic and essential tips about cooking curry. (The books I bought are in 'Useful References', page 266.)

I would like to pass these tips to you for when you try the recipes in this book, or try a recipe of your own. A reasonable curry is not hard, but it just requires a little knowledge and preparation.

1) Curries are made up of two or three groups of ingredients. These groups I indicate when I list the ingredients in the recipe so that it makes it easier for you. Prepare each group, placing all the ingredients in that group together in its own bowl.

2) Preparation is essential, since the addition of all the ingredients is usually very rapid and in a specific order, followed by a period of slow cooking. Always prepare the groups of ingredients as it explains in the method of the recipe.

3) Invest in good ingredients: raw coconut oil is expensive relative to other oils, but it is worth it just for making curry and dal (lentil based dishes), although it can be used anytime and in sweet baking too. Obtainable now in supermarkets.

4) Try to keep your spices and seeds/pods, fresh in airtight containers and in small amounts. Ground spices especially are prone to losing their intensity of flavour and heat quite quickly compared to the whole seeds before grinding. Buying the seeds and grinding them yourself in a coffee grinder is a superb way or preparing spices and enjoying their aroma.

5) You need very few things to start with – build from a simple dal, so that you add only one or two new ingredients with each new dal or curry.

6) The secret to really great sauce and flavour is in the first stages of cooking. When the method tells you to add the spices and allow to sizzle to 'bloom' the spices, I understand this to mean the heat from the oil releases the oil in the ground and whole seeds, and stops the powdery feel on the tongue, a signature of badly cooked curry. Seeds should be sizzled until they begin to 'pop'.

7) Please be aware that curry from Indian restaurants in the UK is really not representative of the food eaten by Indian families. There is less oil, cream and meat eaten in authentic Indian cuisine and is therefore far healthier than we are led to believe. The curries I have included are more authentic than restaurant food, and I thank the generous chefs I have been following online for this.

8) Finally, enjoy cooking this wonderful, aromatic, exciting food. It is such a pleasure and the house sings with the exotic mix of ginger, coriander, lime and coconut, and all the other wondrous flavours. Veganism brought me the courage to try Indian cooking – I only wish now that I had started a long time ago.

Cooking Vegan Sponge Cake

I found this the most frustrating food to cook as a vegan, possibly because I had been known as such a good baker of cakes previously. One gets a bit cocky. Then the eggs and the butter and cream get taken away, and you are left with what looks like nothing but a disaster waiting to happen.

However, this is not the case, as a quick whiz through the Sweet Delights section (page 153) will confirm. Cake is better vegan because it is healthier and cruelty-free!

The biggest change is the lack of egg. But there are plenty of options when having to use an alternative. Eggs traditionally provide binding and help with raising and fixing the sponge so that when fully cooked it doesn't collapse on cooling. The following alternatives do what an egg does, but can also provide other things too like more moisture and extra subtle flavourings. I include some alternatives I was recently told about, but not given measurements for:

- **Ener-G Egg Replacer:** 1½ teaspoons to 2 tablespoons liquid replaces one egg. I usually use fruit juice as the liquid rather than plain water.

- **Vegg** replaces egg yolk. 1 teaspoon added with or without liquid as explained on the packet.

- 1 teaspoon of **Baking Powder** to 1 tablespoon **Apple Cider Vinegar or White Distilled Vinegar.** Replaces one egg.

- 1 tablespoon **ground Flax seed** with 3 tablespoons water and whisk in a blender until thick and creamy. Replaces one egg.

- Ripe **Banana** mashed or puréed. Approximately half a banana replaces 1 large egg. It comes with its banana flavour, though.

- Unsweetened **Apple sauce:** 60g / ¼ cup equals one egg. It can also replace margarine and oil in a cake. Adds a nice subtle tart sweetness too.

- **Silken Tofu:** 55g / ¼ cup blended to make creamy and smooth.

- The juice from a can of **Chickpeas** whisked up until it forms peaks is good as an egg white substitute.

- **Vegan Mayonnaise!**

The other secret about adding the egg alternative if it is the powdered form, or has a powder element, is to do it as the last thing you add to the mixture – at least in most cases. This is because the powders usually start working at producing air bubbles as soon as they come into contact with liquid and/or acid in the mixture. The sooner you can get the cake into the oven after the egg alternative has been added, the better.

Also wherever possible I use orange or apple juice in place of water in the ingredients, since juice helps maintain moisture and adds flavour. I use juice to mix with the Ener-G Egg Replacer powder rather than water, for instance.

Sinking Sponge

If your sponge sinks in the middle it could be because it wasn't fully cooked, you had the oven on too high or the cake too high in position in the oven, the tin's sides were far too high for the depth of the cake, or the sponge mixture was too heavy and wet. Or maybe your egg replacer wasn't the right one for the sponge you are making, or wasn't in the correct quantity.

If you get a sinkage, don't fret. Simply turn it upside down while it cools. I often ice the bottom of a cake as if it is the top. If the middle is too raw, cut it out and ice it like a Bundt ring. If you really can't save it, cut off the cooked bits and serve it with fresh fruit and cream – no one would know! Never get down-hearted. Remember cooking for omnivores is easy – yet they get sunken sponges all the time too!

Preparing Oaties for the Oven

I include several 'oatie' recipes in this book and to avoid repeating the same procedure with each set of instructions, I have decided to show this stage of their preparation here.

When you have mixed together all the ingredients for these wonderful energy bars, you need to continue with the following preparation:

On a baking tray, maximum size 38cm x 26cm and lined with parchment/baking paper, tip all of the mixture:

Roughly distribute it across the whole tin, right into the corners:

Then take another piece of parchment and lay it over the surface, as shown, and press using the flat of the hands:

It is important to compress the mixture so that it binds together when cooking to produce the tray bake that can be sliced. When compressed, remove the top piece of parchment and discard:

Place the tray into the oven, on the middle to upper shelf and bake until golden.

Pressing Tofu

Tofu comes in various forms. The one form I use in this book is called **Firm Silken Tofu** and can be found in supermarkets and health food shops. It comes in a carton which you open as instructed on the carton itself.

Firm Silken Tofu has already had some of its water removed but it still contains a lot of water and for most of the recipes I use it in, removal of further moisture improves consistency of the final dish. To do this is very easy and can take between 30 minutes and three hours, depending on the recipe.

Take a clean tea towel, and lay it folded lengthways (so there are at least two layers) onto a plate. Place the unpacked tofu block onto the towel and place the other half of the towel over the tofu and tuck in the sides as if tucking it up in bed! Then place another plate on top of this and pop some books onto it to provide the pressing weight. Not too much weight though or the tofu will just squish flat.

Doing this for just 30-60 minutes reduces the weight of the tofu from 360g to around 220g. I often press two blocks at a time and pop the other block into an airtight container and refrigerate. It keeps for at least a week, probably more, but I always use it within a few days.

Not all recipes require this procedure, so always read the recipe carefully.

Straining Yoghurt

SKILL SET

Most non-dairy yoghurt is runny rather than thick and gloopy, so if you want to thicken it, you simply need to strain some of the water out of it. I do this with the following set-up – a little crude, but it is very effective.

I use muslin squares cut to the size I want. The muslin I order online from any brewers' site. A piece of string, a skirt hanger and a bowl is all that is needed.

I lay the muslin inside the bowl, with its edges hanging around the rim. I pour all the yoghurt into the centre of the muslin. Then I take a piece of string and put it under the muslin overhanging the rim of the bowl and carefully tie and pull it so it gathers the muslin together in the centre. This produces a muslin ball with the loose muslin gathered at the top. This loose muslin is then pegged by the clothes hanger and the whole thing is hung above the bowl.

Gradually as the water is removed the string can be untied and moved further down the muslin ball and tied again – this keeps pressure on the yoghurt and it strains more effectively.

After 12 hours or so, you can take it down and use. If you are using it to make an extra-thick whip, yoghurt tart or other, and further moisture needs removing, then place lots of kitchen towel inside a clean bowl and place the muslin ball inside. Pop in the fridge and leave for another two to three hours. This absorbs a lot more water from the yoghurt. The whole process reduces the yoghurt volume by over half! This is the process I use to make all of my recipes that ask for strained yoghurt.

The Tin Glossary

In this book I use very little cooking 'terminology' because I think it just confuses what is a simple practice, such as calling a water bath a 'Bain Marie'. I am not a trained cook and have not needed such terminology, and feel it does not sit easily in the home kitchen. I do however refer to equipment with specific names at times, since they explain exactly what is intended. They may not be the correct terms, but they serve the purpose.

In this picture is everything I use in the book that I might mention. Of course don't go and buy everything at once – I certainly didn't. It has taken several years of family life to collect all the equipment I have.

Looking at the photo, you will see I have numbered each item and here list the name I give it. It might not be the correct name in culinary terms but it is descriptive and clear.

1) Loaf tins
2) Spring form tins of various size and depth.
3) Loose-bottomed fluted flan tins
4) High-sided, loose-bottomed cake tin
5) Small pudding tins
6) Standard baking sheet/tray
7) Various ramekins
8) Various ovenproof crockery dishes
9) An enamel Pie dish
10) Standard tray bake tin
11) Ovenproof glass dish and plate

SKILL SET

Lining Tins

This might seem obvious to some, but lining different shaped tins can be a challenge if you have never seen it done.

I tend to err towards laziness and simply grease the tin with margarine and then force a piece of baking parchment into it and press it to the base, smoothing out the creases and folds around the edges. As long as you do this neatly and make the corners neat, it works perfectly well. It also provides you with a useful 'bucket' of parchment for lifting out things like breads, large flat sponges and dense fruit cakes. And yes, I do line bread tins as mine are no longer non-stick!

However, if you are aiming for a neat edge to your baked perfection, then the following advice would be better to follow. Certainly with things like a set 'cheesecake' type dessert, a smooth edge does look lovely.

You will need baking paper or parchment and a little margarine to use as 'glue', a pencil and a pair of scissors. There are three types of tin you will come across in this book: a rectangular bread tin, a round high-sided tin (with loose bottom or removable sprung sides) and a tray bake tin. The bread tin does not need lining for bread as they are usually non-stick, although I always grease mine with vegetable oil, but if you use it to make a rectangle cake (such as my Moist Fruit Cake, page 203) then lining the tin helps stop the edges of the cake scorching and aids the removal of the cake from the tin.

Ready-made parchment linings can be purchased for bread tins, rather like the ones for cupcakes, but I prefer to make do, as it saves on money. I cut a piece of parchment large enough to roughly fit inside the tin – this is just as an estimate. Then I smear the inside of the tin with margarine and force the parchment in and press along the bottom. I then align the parchment along the long sides of the tin before cutting a slit into the parchment at the corners from top edge down to the corner of the tin. The parchment can then be overlapped into the corners to make a smooth lining.

A round tin is much easier. Place the tin down on the parchment and draw around the base and cut out. Then take the seam of the tin (the line where the side of the tin joins itself) and lay it down onto the parchment, making a mark with a pencil on the parchment exactly in line with the seam. Then roll the tin on its side along the parchment until you reach the seam again and mark it on the parchment with the pencil. You now have the length of the side of the tin (circumference), and you just need to decide how deep to cut it. Once you have the base and side cut you can smear the tin with margarine and stick the parchment onto the inside of the tin.

For a tray bake tin, I always line it because it is so much easier to get the cake out. Not all cakes can be placed upside down to remove, so having parchment you can hold, to lift the cake out, is very useful indeed. Line a tray bake tin as you would a bread tin.

Even if you are using non-stick tins, it is always best to take the time to line the tins. It makes for better cakes and certainly much easier removal from the tins. It prevents scorching of sponges that are in the oven a long time.

Lentils: A Vegan Staple?

For many the very word 'lentil' brings with it horrifying images of green and brown gloop, mushy and flavourless, yet I have learnt that they can be a comforting and very yummy addition to dishes – if you know what to do with them!

There are whole books devoted to lentils, there are so many varieties. My favourite use of them is as Dal, an Indian staple dish eaten at nearly every meal, made primarily of lentils, spiced and mixed with various vegetables. Dal is like the British version of bread and butter at every meal. This, a practice of the war generation, was certainly true of my grandparents. It was always a treat at the end of Sunday tea to get the left-over slice of bread and butter and sprinkle it with sugar!

The reason lentils are used is because they are fabulously nutritious and full of fibre. So try to include them at least once a week. They are not absolutely essential to a vegan diet, but they help a great deal.

The lentils I stick to in this book are red lentils – that little split orange pea we used to blow down straws at each other in school – the yellow (Chana Dal) lentil, a split yellow pea which takes a lot longer to cook than the red lentil, although there is a petite yellow split pea called Mung Dal which cooks far quicker, and the green or brown varieties. To start with, though, the red and the yellow (Chana) are the best. They have a fresh and mild flavour. Others range from an earthy to a peppery taste.

This is very important. You **must rinse lentils thoroughly** before cooking. A white powder comes off them and turns the water milky. There will also be grit and other miscellaneous bits that you find surfacing as you rinse them. Do it in a bowl, rubbing the lentils between your palms, then straining and re-filling the bowl with water. I do this at least five times until the water is virtually clear.

Soaking lentils is a good habit too as it facilitates faster cooking. The Red lentil won't need soaking. It softens in around 20-25 minutes. But the Yellow can take up to three hours. In traditional Indian cooking this is never a problem. Their dishes will simmer literally all day, at least before the invention of the slow cooker, hence the incredible rich, deep flavours they achieve.

I have noticed that if I try cooking lentils in fluids other than water, they take a lot longer to cook. This is especially true with the Chana Dal. Bear this in mind when working out cooking times. Although I like dal made with milk, I tend to cook the harder, larger lentils in water first.

Mushrooms: Friend or Foe?

It is worth a moment to let you in on my feelings about mushrooms, in case you yourself dislike or avoid them. They appear in quite a few of my dishes.

I was never a great fan of them in my omnivorous days and my children hated the smell of them. I only used them fried with bacon and eggs, and their flavour was always very distinct. I hasten to add I never boiled them – a travesty of an end to any mushroom! And I never peel them. But I never really gave the mushroom a chance to shine.

Once I decided to include mushrooms as a source of protein and vitamins in our diet, I realised that mushrooms are as much a flavouring and enrichment to dishes as a dried tomato or a stock cube might be – you wouldn't want to eat one on its own, but in a dish they add something satisfyingly yummy. Then once you unlock the beauty of their flavour you actually use them as the key or star ingredient, in the place of meat itself.

If it is the texture that puts you off, again, that was my problem. But I have really persevered and now find I love mushrooms cooked in various ways and as an addition to many things. My kids also feel the same way, although none of us like them raw – we draw the line there.

So whatever your own feelings about the mushrooms please try them in the dishes I have selected for this book. Mushrooms are of great benefit in any kitchen and provide a lot of nutrition. Briefly I use these:

- **Mini White Closed Cup**: sweet mild flavour and pale inside.
- **Large Closed Cup**: sweet, slightly more fleshy than the mini ones with a distinct pale brown colour to the inside (the gills).

- **White Open Cup**: these vary in colour and have a slightly stronger sweet/savoury flavour.
- **Chestnut Mushrooms**: small and large, these have a slightly nutty flavour and a firmer flesh than the white mushrooms. A great all-rounder, they make wonderful mushroom sauce.
- **Mini Portabella Mushrooms**: very flavourful with a slightly sweet-of-the-woods sort of flavour, with dark, almost black underside (gills) which will colour the food they cook with. Delicate fleshiness that is quite narrow, so slices look like umbrellas.
- **Large Portabella Mushrooms**: really flavourful of-the-woods and fleshy with real substance, so if not over-cooked give a satisfying bulk and flavour to dishes. Great whole. Will stain gravy and juices dark to black.
- **Exotic Mushrooms**: for this book I have steered clear of these. But give them a whirl if you like. Many are of Japanese origin and are fashionable on the restaurant circuit, such as the Shiitake mushroom.

NOTES

Oven Temperature Conversion

Celsius / Fan	Fahrenheit	Gas Mark
110 / 90	225	¼
120 / 100	250	½
140 / 120	275	1
150 / 130	300	2
160 / 140	325	3
180 / 160	350	4
190 / 170	375	5
200 / 180	400	6
220 / 200	425	7
230 / 210	450	8
240 / 220	475	9

English Across the Pond

UK English	American English
Baking Parchment	Wax paper
Baking Powder	Baking Soda plus Cream of Tartar
Baking Soda	Baking Soda
Biscuit	Cookie
Spring Onions	Scallions/Green Onions
Caster Sugar	Superfine Sugar
Chips	Fries
Cling-film	Saran wrap
Corn Flour	Corn Starch
Courgette	Zucchini
Coriander leaves	Cilantro
Coriander Seeds	Coriander
Demerara Sugar	Light brown cane sugar
Digestive Biscuit	Used like Graham Crackers
Frying Pan	Skillet
Grill	Grill / Broiler
Icing	Frosting
Icing Sugar	Confectioner's Sugar
Jam	Jelly
Jelly	Jello
Pastry case	Pie case
Pie (savoury)	Pot Pie
Plain Flour	All-Purpose Flour
Porridge	Oatmeal
Pudding / Sweet	Dessert
Spring Greens	Collard Greens (similar)
Stone (in fruit)	Pit
Swede	Rutabaga
Sweetcorn	Corn / Maize
Tart	Pie (shallow)
Veg Suet	Veg Shortening / shredded white fat

NOTES

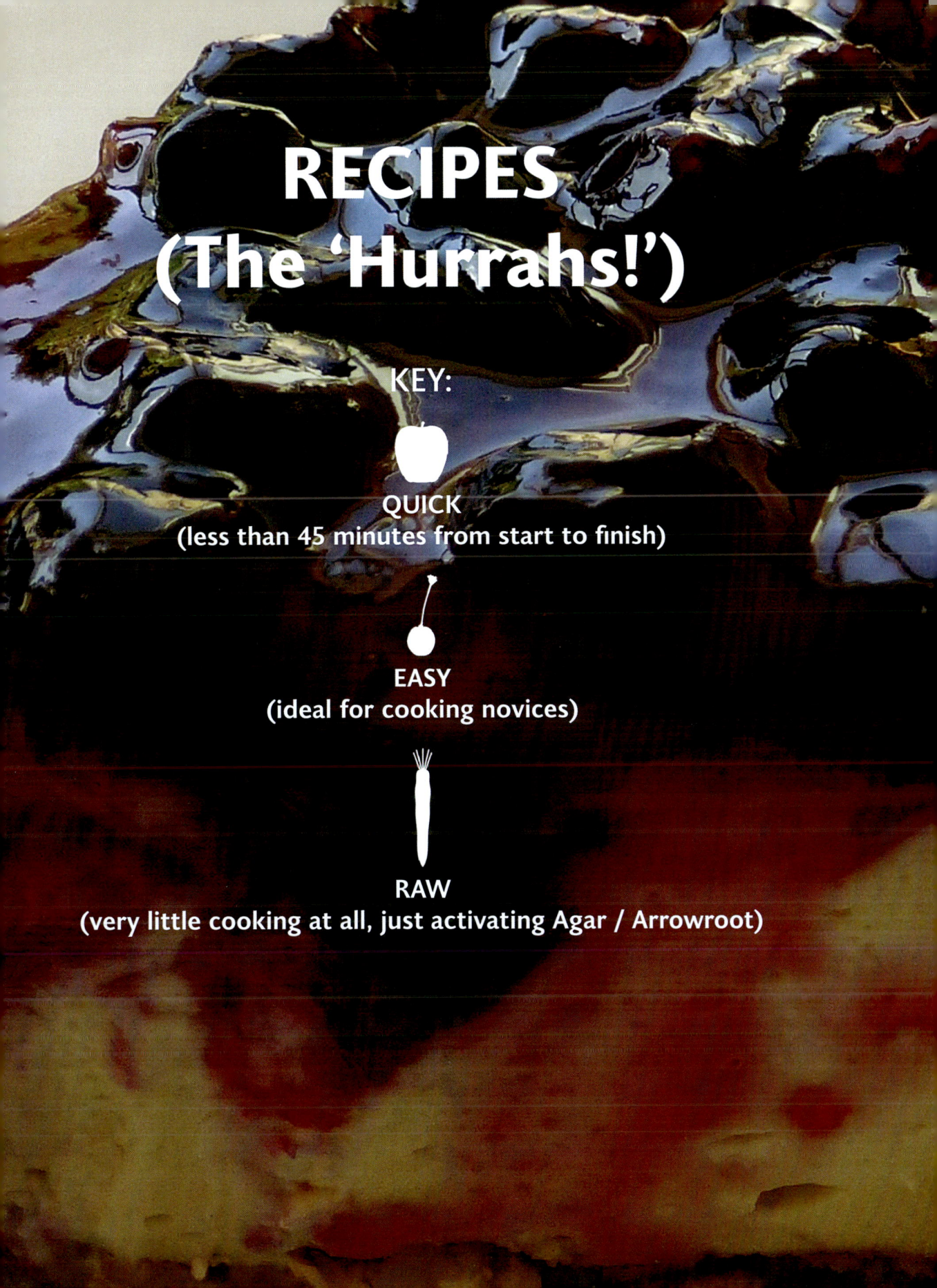

RECIPES
(The 'Hurrahs!')

KEY:

QUICK
(less than 45 minutes from start to finish)

EASY
(ideal for cooking novices)

RAW
(very little cooking at all, just activating Agar / Arrowroot)

SOUP, STOCK & BREAD

ALL SEASON SOUP

TRADITIONAL CASSEROLED VEGETABLE STOCK

I make this when I already have the oven cooking something else.

Time: Prep 20 minutes, cooking 90 minutes at 130°C. Makes 2½ pints / 1.5 litres

- 3 pints / 2 litres Boiling Water
- Salt & Pepper
- 2 Onions
- 2 cloves Garlic
- 1 Bell Pepper
- 1 Courgette
- 2 large Carrots
- ½ cup Pearl Barley
- ½ tablespoon Paprika
- ½ tablespoon dried Herbs
- 1 tablespoon Tomato Purée
- 1 teaspoon Marmite (or ½ tablespoon Dark Soya Sauce)
- ¼ cup Red Wine
- Bay leaf
- ½ teaspoon Mustard

Place all of the ingredients into a casserole pot and pop in oven on low setting for 90 minutes minimum. The slow cooking over a long period of time allows all the flavours to be released and all of the ingredients to soften.

Once cooked, remove the bay leaves and blitz the ingredients to a rough liquid, and strain through a sieve, catching all of the liquid stock in a bowl. You will have to do this in a few stages, using a spoon to keep stirring the stock as it goes through the sieve. The remaining vegetable mash in the sieve can be discarded.

Once all of the stock has been strained you may want to strain it again through a finer sieve, but I like the gravy to have some of the fine pulp which does disappear once gravy is made.

Pour the stock into individual containers so that you can freeze in portions and use as you wish. I tend to freeze them in portions that will make gravy for two people.

This is a rich stock which will be added to depending what it is used for in the recipe.

STOVE-TOP AROMATIC VEGETABLE STOCK

Some of the liquid will be lost using this method.

Time: 20 minutes prep, 1½ to 2 hours simmer

- 2 Ripe Tomatoes
- 1 large stick Celery
- 1 large Carrot
- 1 Bell Pepper
- 2 Onions

- 2 Bay leaves
- 4-6 crushed green Cardamom Pods
- ½ teaspoon Sea Salt
- Handful of Pearl Barley
- 2–3 pints boiling water

Simply chop everything coarsely and place in a large stockpot. Bring to the boil and then set on lowest heat setting, place the lid on the pot and leave to simmer very gently for 1½ to 2 hours or more.

Remove the bay leaves and cardamom pods and blitz roughly before straining it through a colander and then again through a sieve. Allow to cool and freeze in portions for use later.

Remember you can flavour your stock with anything you like. You may even want to make stock using the trimmings from cabbage, cauliflower, sprouts, skins from carrots, parsnips and the stringy pieces of celery that don't get eaten. It is a great way to use what we often throw away.

This stock will be enriched with further ingredients depending what it is used for, and will be thickened with cornflour or similar as needed.

AROMATIC VEGETABLE SOUP

Time: 20 minutes prep, 30 minutes cooking. Serves 3–4

1½ pt. / 850ml Vegetable Stock
½ cup Red Lentils
1 clove Garlic
1 cm fresh Ginger
2 medium Carrots
5–6 Spring Onions
½ tablespoon soft Brown Sugar
1 tablespoon Tomato Purée

1 tablespoon Light Soya Sauce
⅓ bulb of Fennel (or teaspoon of Ground Fennel Seeds)
½ Bell Pepper
½ a Chilli or dried equivalent (optional)
Salt & Pepper
Fresh Flat Leaf Parsley
2 tablespoons Non-Dairy Margarine (or Raw Coconut Oil)

1) Chop all the ingredients as finely or roughly as you wish. The final soup can be blended if required or left rustic.

2) Place in a large saucepan with a lid, the margarine (or oil) and melt. Add to it the onion, garlic and ginger and allow to sizzle gently until soft and the onions begin to brown.

3) Add the stock and all of the rest of the ingredients. Bring to the boil then simmer gently with the lid on for around 30 minutes, until the lentils are soft.

4) Serve hot as is, or add cream, or blitz smooth.

Freezes well.

Tip: For a winter alternative add some pearl barley or a mixture of lentils and beans remembering to add a little more stock.

Tip: This is a good soup for those that have been poorly and need to eat light, easily digestible foods. With the added ginger it also calms the stomach.

MOROCCAN STYLE LENTIL SOUP

Having eaten a tinned soup named 'Moroccan Chickpea' and liked the flavour, I tried my own version, replacing the chickpeas for lentils, which I personally prefer. You could use any pulse you choose.

Time: 20 minutes prep, 30–40 minutes cooking. Serves 3–4

- 1¼ pints / 700ml Vegetable Stock
- 2 tablespoons Non-Dairy Margarine
- 2 Onions
- 2 cloves Garlic
- 5 chopped Plum Tomatoes
- 1 cup Red Lentils (or your choice)
- 1 tablespoon Tomato Purée
- 1 Bay Leaf
- 1 teaspoon Garam Masala (or ½ tsp ground Cumin plus ½ tsp ground Coriander)
- ½ teaspoon ground Fennel Seeds or dried Tarragon
- ½ teaspoon dried crushed Chillies (this will give medium-hot soup)
- 1 teaspoon Paprika
- Salt and Pepper
- 1 inch of Cinnamon Bark / Stick
- ¼pt / 150ml Non-Dairy milk or cream
- Any left-over beans or peas can be added.

1) Whatever lentils you choose, make sure you rinse them fully if they are raw, until the water from them runs clear. When lentils are prepared leave them aside until ready to add to the pot.

2) Melt the margarine in a saucepan with a lid and add the onion, garlic, tomatoes and all the herbs and seasonings, and allow to sizzle for 3–4 minutes.

3) Pour in the vegetable stock, lentils, tomato purée and bay leaf. Bring to the boil, then with the lid on, simmer briskly for ten minutes, then turn down the heat and simmer gently until the lentils are soft. This may take longer if you use a different lentil and you may need a little extra water, so make sure you don't let the soup get too dry. Always read the instructions on the lentil packet as many lentils differ.

4) Once cooked, remove the bay leaf, add the cream and with a hand blender blitz to your desired texture. If you wish to add beans, peas or the like I would add these at the end, pre-cooked, so they keep their shape and colour.

Freezes well.

AROMATIC CURRIED LENTIL SOUP (WITH NAAN-INSPIRED FLAT BREAD)

AROMATIC CURRIED LENTIL SOUP

On a cold night, a curried dish of anything is so unbelievably comforting. This is one of our winter staples.

Time: 2 hours soaking, prep and cook 40 minutes

- 1 tablespoon oil or Non-Dairy Margarine
- 1 large clove Garlic, diced
- 1 large Onion, diced
- 1 cm Ginger, peeled and diced finely
- Stem of fresh Rosemary, finely chopped
- 3 Cardamom pods, slightly crushed
- 1 tablespoon of mild or medium Curry Powder
- Juice ½ Lemon
- 1 cup Lentils, rinsed thoroughly and soaked in boiling water for 2 hours
- 500g Passata (sieved plum tomatoes)
- 500ml Water (or vegetable stock)
- Salt & pepper
- 1 tablespoon Dark Soya Sauce
- Any odd bits of veg left in fridge, finely diced
- Optional – Non-Dairy single cream

1) Put oil/margarine in a big lidded saucepan, and heat. Add the first eight ingredients in the list. Allow to sizzle for 3–4 minutes, stirring continually.

2) Add the soaked and drained lentils and stir and simmer for a minute before adding all of the other ingredients including the water or vegetable stock.

3) Bring the liquid to the boil and rapidly simmer for 10 minutes. Then turn down to simmer gently with the lid on, until the lentils are soft but not mushy. Time taken will depend on type of lentils used. Read their packaging for this.

4) With a hand blender blitz the soup, but only partly. This thickens it and gives it a pleasant texture. You may wish to blend completely for a smooth soup, but whole lentils have a lovely feel and the texture gives the soup its heartiness. I always add cream last. Stir in, re-warm and serve. Freezes well and is even nice cold as a dip.

Tip: This can be used as a side dish, like a dal, when eating curry or with rice and bread. Adding more lentils and garlic will produce a good thick dal. Spinach can also be added.

SOUP, STOCK & BREAD

CREAM OF CELERIAC SOUP

If you have never tasted celeriac before then this is a really lovely taste sensation you should try. Slightly peppery, with aniseed and celery tones, it has a beautiful white subtle flesh beneath its rough, leathery-looking coat. I was surprised by it and liked how different it was from any other soup I had made up to that point. It is also very light and soft, a texture that would work all year round.

Time: 15 minutes prep and 15 minutes cooking. Serves 3–4

3 tablespoons Olive Oil
3 tablespoons Non-Dairy Margarine
1 small Onion
1 small clove Garlic
½ cm fresh Ginger
1 whole Celeriac
2 cups cooking water (including the water the celeriac was parboiled in)

3–5 leaves fresh Sage
One Bay leaf
5 stalks Coriander
Salt and pepper
2 tablespoons White Wine
½ cup Non-Dairy Single Cream

1) Peel the celeriac and slice into cubes about the size of a sugar lump. Cover with water and bring to the boil. Turn off the heat and let the pan stand while you prepare the rest of the ingredients.

2) Put the oil, margarine, onion, garlic and ginger into a small frying pan and gently heat to soften. Do not let them caramelise.

3) Strain the celeriac, keeping the water. Measure out 2 cups of this water and place into a large saucepan. You may need to add extra tap water to make up the amount required.

4) Into the saucepan add the celeriac and all the other ingredients, except for the cream. Make sure the herbs are finely chopped, apart from the bay leaf which will be removed later.

5) Bring to the boil, then turn down heat and simmer gently for around 15 minutes. Check the celeriac is soft.

6) Remove the bay leaf, add the cream and with a hand blender blitz until smooth. Taste to check if extra seasoning is required.

CREAM OF TOMATO SOUP

Time: 40 minutes Serves 4–8 depending on whether you dilute the recipe

1 tablespoon Non-Dairy Margarine

2 large Carrots, grated

1 medium-large Onion

1–2 Garlic cloves

2 Sun-dried Tomato halves

3 pinches Sea Salt and Pepper

1 teaspoon dried Basil

½ teaspoon dried Tarragon

500g box Passata (sieved plum tomatoes) or half this amount if you want less richness.

1 cup water

300–350g Non-Dairy Single Cream

1) Melt the margarine in a large saucepan with a lid, and gently sauté the onion and garlic.

2) Add the rest of the ingredients and bring to the boil. Simmer gently for 20 minutes, then blitz with a hand blender until smooth. Taste and adjust to your liking.

Tip: Great as a pasta sauce in its concentrated state.

SOUP, STOCK & BREAD

SUN-DRIED TOMATO TEA SOUP

SUN-DRIED TOMATO TEA SOUP

Inspired by Nigel Slater, I decided to have a go at making a 'tea' soup, named because of its colour. Nigel used dried shiitake mushrooms; I used sun-dried tomatoes.

Time: 1 hour minimum soak and prep, cooking 15 minutes. Serves 2

8 Sun-dried Tomato halves	1 Celery stick
2 whole Cloves	1 tablespoon White Cooking Wine
½ Lime, juiced, and some Lemon zest	½ Red Bell Pepper
1 tablespoon Tomato paste	¼ cup mini Pasta
1 tablespoon Agave Nectar	Teaspoon dried Tarragon
1 cm fresh Ginger	¾ pint / 300ml Boiling Water
2 Spring Onions	

1) Place the tomatoes (pulled out thin and sliced roughly), lime juice, agave nectar, peeled and chopped ginger and whole cloves into a bowl with the boiling water, cover and leave to stand for 1 hour, longer if you can. I leave mine for the morning and make the soup for lunch. Stir occasionally.

2) Chop the pepper, celery and spring onion very small as these will remain virtually raw and the soup needs to look delicate. Use all of the onions and the celery as the green parts add intensity of flavour and colour.

3) Strain the tomato liquid. Take two of the tomatoes and the ginger and dice them up, retaining the other tomatoes for another recipe. Put the liquid and the diced tomatoes and ginger into a saucepan, and add the mini pasta shapes. Bring to the boil and simmer until pasta is nearly cooked.

4) Add the chopped vegetables, the wine, tomato paste and some lemon zest and taste. If you like a little chilli heat, add some now. Add a little sugar or salt depending on your taste.

5) Continue simmering and stirring now until the pasta is cooked.

Tip: This soup tastes better if it is left for a day in the fridge and re-heated as the flavours become intense and blended. Serve with a slice of lime and some crunchy bread. It is nice cold too.

PEA & ROASTED PARSNIP SOUP

PEA & ROASTED PARSNIP SOUP

Very green and very sweet. Can be cooked without the parsnips, with extra peas or spinach instead.

Time: 50 minutes Oven 200°C for roasting parsnips

- 3–4 Parsnips (enough to give 150g when cooked)
- 200g Frozen Peas (petits pois)
- 50g Raw Baby Spinach
- 250ml Vegetable Stock
- Salt if required
- 150ml Non-Dairy Milk (not needed if you are making this as a thick dip)
- ½ Lime, juiced
- Cream and Lemon / Orange zest to decorate

1) Peel the parsnips and cut into chunks. Roast for 30–40 minutes in a little oil in a hot oven, taking care to avoid them burning, so not too high in the oven. Cover with foil if necessary.

2) Once parsnips are cooked, place in a blender with all of the other ingredients and blitz until smooth. Taste and adjust seasoning as required.

Tip: This is great as a dip. Just don't add the milk.

ALL SEASON SOUP

A satisfying crunch to some of the ingredients makes this extra refreshing and yummy.

Time: 15 minutes prep, 15 minutes cooking. Serves 4

3 Bell Peppers
600ml / 1 pint Vegetable Stock
3 medium Onions
5–6 sticks Celery
2 tablespoons White Cooking Wine
1 tablespoon Tomato Purée
1 tablespoon Light Soya Sauce
Handful of grain, pre-cooked (Pearl Barley or Wheatberries, for instance)
1 tablespoon Non-Dairy Margarine

Bay leaf
¼ teaspoon dried crushed Chillies or Cajun Spice (optional)
1–2 tablespoons Agave Nectar (or similar honey substitute)
¼ teaspoon Salt
½ teaspoon dried Basil, Tarragon, Garlic Salt, Thyme and Paprika (if you don't have all of these, just use what you have)
1 tablespoon Lemon juice
1 tablespoon Cornflour

1) Put your chosen grain on to cook.

2) Peel, seed and dice the vegetables up very fine.

3) Place vegetable stock into a large lidded saucepan and add the vegetables you have chopped.

4) Add all of the other ingredients except for the margarine, agave nectar and cornflour.

5) Bring to the boil and then simmer for no more than 12–15 minutes. You want the vegetables to still have a little crunch to them if possible. (If you are going to keep this and serve later, then re-heating will cook them again, so cook for less time now. Same if you are freezing the soup.)

6) Place the cooked grain and margarine into the soup and stir. Taste and add the agave nectar to sweeten as you like it. Add salt and pepper if you wish.

7) Now to thicken: I like my soup to be thick enough that it carries the vegetables, rather than they drop to the floor of your soup bowl and all you have left is a watery pond! But this is personal preference. Mix the cornflour in a cup with a little cold water and add bit by bit to the soup, stirring it vigorously to avoid lumping. It will begin thickening straight away so you can easily tell when you have it right.

Serve this with bread or dumplings depending on the season.

FOCACCIA (ITALIAN BREAD)

This is such a pleasure to eat. An Italian-style bread which we sometimes end up just eating with some nuts and an onion salad or potatoes while it is still warm. It toasts well too – melts in the mouth.

Time: total 3 hours 45 minutes, including the 25 minutes cooking time. Oven 200°C middle shelf

1¼ teaspoons / 7g Dried Active Yeast
1¼ cups / 300ml warm Water
1 teaspoon Sugar
3½ cups / 500g White Bread Flour
1 teaspoon Sea Salt

5 tablespoons Olive Oil
2 teaspoons dried Herbs (try Tarragon, Marjoram and Basil together)
3–6 halves Sun-dried Tomatoes and / or 8–12 black Olives (optional)

1) Prep the yeast: in a jug place the warm water, sugar and yeast. Whisk briskly and leave in a draft-free corner covered with a plate. Leave until 1–2cm of froth has appeared. (Note that if froth does not appear inside 15 minutes, or it is very meagre, it could be one of three things: you forgot the sugar, the water is too hot or too cold, or the yeast is old. Discard and start again.)

2) Place the rest of the ingredients in a large mixing bowl, but keep back 2 tablespoons of the olive oil. Make sure you chop the tomatoes and/or the olives finely so they are able to be thoroughly distributed throughout the loaf.

3) When the yeast is ready, stir it and add all of it to the flour mix in the bowl. Stir with a spoon or your hands until the liquid is soaked up.

4) Tip the mixture onto a floured surface and push together into a ball. Using plenty of flour as you go, knead the bread for 10 minutes. If you have never kneaded bread before, don't worry. Simply take one side of the dough and bring across diagonally and push it down into the other side of the dough, then repeat using the other side, pulling across and pressing down. Use the heel of the palm to press down and try to get into a rhythm. It gets easier as you do it because kneading is stretching out the protein in the flour, making it more 'elastic'. After ten minutes you should feel quite tired and the dough should feel much softer. This stage is the most important and you will get better with practice.

5) Fashion the dough into a ball and put into a large bowl or plastic container, cover with a damp tea cloth and leave in a warm place for 2 hours. I heat my oven slightly then turn it off and use that as a warming cupboard as we don't have an airing cupboard like my Nan had.

6) After 2 hours the bread will have tripled or quadrupled in size and now needs to be kneaded for 2 more minutes and placed into its baking tin. I like to use a high sided cake tin as it gives a deep round loaf which is very attractive and soft inside.

7) Once in its tin, punch it down and press your knuckles or fingertips firmly into the surface to make little pits. Take the remaining olive oil (that 2 tablespoons you kept back earlier), and drizzle all over the dough surface, then with your fingers work it into the pits. Sprinkle some coarse salt and pepper on top and leave in a warm place for another hour. This time you need to use some clear film loosely over the dough to allow it to rise again without restriction and to keep it damp. Keep in the warm.

8) The dough will not rise as much as it did before but now it is ready for baking.

9) Pop on middle shelf and bake for 25 minutes so the top is golden all over.

Freezes well.

Tip: This is great sliced, popped under the grill topped with tomatoes, basil and mayo.

Tip: This is extra lovely if you replace the cup of water with half almond milk and half water, or any similar milk. It gives an even softer dough.

FOCACCIA (ITALIAN BREAD)

BASIC FLAT BREAD

This is very useful to be able to make as it is versatile, very quick and goes with anything – oh, and is healthy. Use any sort of flour, combination of herbs, seeds, dried tomatoes, olives or whatever you can find. Leave them whole or slice into strips. Ideal for snacks, picnics and lunch boxes.

2 cups Plain Flour (or bread flour)
½ cup cold water
Pinch Salt
1½ teaspoons Baking Powder
Oil for frying

1) Mix all ingredients together with your fingers and fashion into a ball of dough. This should be a little sticky but not enough to break off all over your fingers. Add more flour if this happens.

2) Divide into two portions and roll out on floured surface until the dough is pretty thin, as if it were short crust pastry. Experiment with this, though. Too thin and it won't puff up and will be leathery. Too thick and it is heavy and slightly doughy in the middle.

3) Put a little oil into a frying pan and place one portion of the rolled out dough into it. Cook until golden on the underside and little pockets of air are forming on the top side. Then flip over. Cook for another minute making sure it doesn't burn.

Tip: These make good pizza bases.

NAAN INSPIRED FLAT BREAD

After having unsuccessfully attempted to make authentic Naan bread using yoghurt and the traditional method of finger-stirring wet runny dough to thicken (but it never did), I decided to have a go creating something that was easier and quick but still gave me a Naan bread kick of flavour. This is it!

Time: 15 minutes prep (30 minutes chilling if you have time); 15 minutes frying for four mini breads

- 2 cups Plain or Self Raising Flour (this makes the lightest breads, but you can add other flours if you wish)
- 1½ teaspoons Baking Powder
- 1 tablespoon soft Brown Sugar
- Generous pinch coarse Sea Salt, slightly ground
- Pepper
- 1 tablespoon Nigella Seeds
- ½ tablespoon Fennel seeds
- 2 tablespoon Non-Dairy cream or Yoghurt
- ½ cup cold water
- A little Oil for frying

1) Into a mixing bowl place all of the dry ingredients and mix well together.

2) Now add the wet ingredients and with your fingers stir together. Fashion it into a ball of slightly sticky dough. You may need to add more water or yoghurt if you are using wholemeal, malt or seeded flours as these are dryer. The dough must be sticky.

3) Chill, wrapped in cling film, for 30 minutes before frying if you can. This seems to make the dough softer and fluffier when fried.

4) Split the dough into either 2, 4 or 6 portions depending on how large or small you want the breads. Four portions are the size of a side plate each.

5) With your hands and a little flour press the dough portion out flat. Use palm and finger tips to get the shape you want and aim to make them about ½ cm thick. This is something you will get right with a little practice. Making four breads means making them a side plate size, or as six breads, saucer sized. You can roll with a pin but I find this compresses the dough too much.

6) With a half a tablespoon of oil in a hot frying pan, add the flattened dough and fry for a couple of minutes until you see air bubbles forming in the dough surface. Once the underneath has gone golden, flip over and cook for another 1–2 minutes. Make sure the heat is not too high or the bread will scorch.

Tip: Eat whilst hot by breaking apart with your hands and dip into your dal or curry or Ratatouille or whatever you like! Great on their own as a snack, on a picnic or in a lunchbox. Best eaten the day they are made.

MULTI SEED BLOOMER

Time: 2 hours rising, 10 minutes kneading, 25–30 minutes cooking. Oven 200–210°C middle shelf

7g / 1¼ teaspoon Dried Active Yeast plus 280ml warm water plus one teaspoon sugar

500g / 1lb 4 oz Bread Flour of your choice (I use a Country Grain mix or similar)

1 teaspoon Salt

2 tablespoons Vegetable Oil

½ cup / handful extra seeds optional

1) Prep the yeast: in a bowl or jug, place the sugar into the water and then the yeast and whisk with a fork. Pop a plate over the bowl/jug and place in a draught-free position for 15 minutes or until there is around 1-2 cm froth. If there is no froth, then one of three things has occurred: either the water was too hot or cold, you forgot the sugar or the yeast is old. Discard and start again.

2) Place all the other ingredients into a large mixing bowl. Once yeast is ready add to the flour and mix together with hands or spoon until liquid has gone.

3) Tip the messy mixture onto a floured surface and bring together firmly with hands. If it is very sticky and sticking to hands, keep adding sprinklings of flour until this stops happening.

4) Knead for 10 minutes. Kneading is easy but tiring. Take one side of the dough and pull diagonally over and press it down with the heal of your palm. Then take the other side of the dough with your other hand and repeat the other way. Get a rhythm going and with practise this will soften the dough and make it elastic.

5) A bloomer loaf is cooked without being inside a tin, so a baking tray (or any large flat oven dish) is used, making sure there is plenty of room for the dough to swell three times its original size in all directions. Cover with a damp cloth and allow to rise for 2 hours in a warm place. I cover mine in a way that prevents the cloth actually touching the dough as it tends to stick. You can use bottles on the baking tray to use as 'scaffolding' for the cloth.

6) Leave it covered until it is ready to go into the oven which needs to be hot. Bake for 25–30 minutes.

7) When you remove the loaf, remove it from the tin immediately onto a cooling rack. The bread is cooked if it sounds hollow when you tap the bottom.

Freezes well.

SUN-DRIED TOMATO & PUMPKIN SEED BREAD

A favourite bread of ours for its nutritional value as well as its pretty texture and nutty flavour: a lovely dense moist bread, fabulous toasted the next day. One of the nicest slices of toast with strong orange marmalade or raspberry jam. Freezes well.

Time: 2 hours rising time, 10 minutes kneading, 25–30 minutes cooking. Oven 200–210°C middle shelf

- 7g / 1¼ teaspoon Dried Active Yeast plus 280ml warm water plus one teaspoon sugar
- 500g / 1lb 4 oz Bread Flour (mix of ⅓ white to ⅔ other)
- 1¼ teaspoons Salt (less if you want low sodium)
- 2 tablespoons Vegetable Oil
- ½ cup / handful Pumpkin Seeds (or other)
- 4–6 halves Sun-dried Tomatoes (NOT the ones in oil), finely diced

1) Prep the yeast: in a bowl or jug, place the sugar into the water and then the yeast and whisk with a fork. Pop a plate over the bowl/jug and place in a draught free position for 15 minutes or until there is around 1–2 cm froth. If no froth appears then one of three things has occurred: either the water is too hot or cold, you forgot the sugar or the yeast is old. Discard and start again.

2) Place all the other ingredients into a large mixing bowl. Once yeast is ready add to the flour and mix together with hands or spoon until liquid has been absorbed.

3) Tip the messy mixture onto a floured surface and bring together firmly with hands. If it is very sticky and sticking to hands, keep adding sprinklings of flour until this stops happening. You will probably need to do this throughout the first 5 minutes of kneading.

4) Knead for 10 minutes. Simply take the side of the dough, pull it over diagonally to the other side and press down with the heal of your palm. Then repeat using your other hand going across the other way. Continue trying to get into a rhythm. It gets easier with practice. It should tire you and make the dough softer and more pliable.

5) Place the softer dough, fashioned into a neat ball, into the bread or high sided cake tin. Cover with a damp cloth and allow it to rise for 2 hours in a warm place. I use bottles on a baking sheet as scaffolding for the cloth so that it doesn't touch the rising dough, as it will stick.

6) The dough will triple in size. Leave it covered until it is ready to go into the oven which needs to be hot. Bake for 25–30 minutes.

7) When you remove the loaf, tip it out immediately onto a cooling rack. The bread is cooked if it sounds hollow when you tap the bottom.

PATÉ, SPREADS & SAUCES

Salads, Sides, Dressing & Gravy

MAYONNAISE

RICH TOMATO, PEPPER & MUSHROOM SAUCE

Time: 20 minutes Makes approx. 600ml sauce

3 tablespoons Olive Oil (or other)
1 Onion
1 clove Garlic
6–8 Button Mushrooms (or similar)
1½ Bell Peppers
Salt & Pepper
¼ teaspoon Mustard
½ teaspoon dried Basil

Juice of a small Lemon
300–400ml Passata (sieved plum tomatoes)
½ tablespoon Tomato Purée
1 teaspoon dried Herbs
½ teaspoon dried Tarragon
¼ teaspoon Chilli powder (or crushed dried chillies)
Dash of Dark Soya Sauce
½ teaspoon Cyder Vinegar

1) Place oil into a frying pan and gently fry together the chopped onion, garlic, mushrooms and peppers until soft.

2) Place these softened ingredients into a blender.

3) Add to the blender all of the other ingredients and blend until smooth.

4) You may wish to add red wine, sweet chestnuts or fresh Rosemary to enrich the flavour further.

Tip: You can make a raw version by simply not frying at the beginning.

SWEET CHILLI RED WINE SAUCE

Time: 20 minutes. Makes approx. 600ml

- 4 tablespoons Olive Oil
- 2 large Bell Peppers (skinned)
- 2 strong White Onions
- 3 cloves Garlic
- 300ml Passata
- 1 tablespoon Sherry Vinegar (or similar)
- 2 tablespoons Red Wine
- ¼ teaspoon Salt
- ½ teaspoon fresh chopped Rosemary
- 1 tablespoon Soft Brown Sugar (or 2 tbsp Agave)
- ½ tablespoon Paprika
- ½ tablespoon Mild or Hot Chilli Powder
- 1 teaspoon dried Tarragon
- 6–8 Prunes
- ⅓–½ cup / 80–120ml Non-Dairy Milk

1) If you want this raw, simply take all of the ingredients and blend together.

2) If you want it as I like it, then simply use one tablespoon of the olive oil to fry and brown the onion and garlic before adding to the processor or blender.

3) To skin a bell pepper simply cut open and de-seed, then lay skin upwards and grill on a hot grill until the skin goes black and mottled. Then place the hot peppers in a bowl of cold water. The skin will peel off easily. The blacker the skins the easier they peel.

This sauce can be heated or used cold.

Keeps chilled in an air-tight container for up to a week.

ROAST POTATOES

If you can cook great roast potatoes, and make a rich gravy then you will win the hearts of your family even if the meat is missing from their Sunday Roast plates. Make potatoes the centre of the meal, fluffy in the middle and crunchy on the outside, with a hint of Rosemary, Sage and Salt.

Time: Some prep time and 45–60 minutes roasting time. Oven middle to upper shelf 200°C

White Potatoes (and / or Sweet Potatoes) – NOT new ones

Dried Herbs (Rosemary, Thyme, Sage)

Salt and Pepper

Olive Oil and vegetable oil

1) Turn on your oven, placing the shelf high. Peel and cut up your potatoes so that they are the size of a clementine – in other words not too big. I find roasties work best when there is plenty of crunchy surface area to fluffy middle.

2) Rinse them and place in a pan, just covered over with cold water. Then bring to the boil. Turn down to simmer.

3) You need to cook the potatoes until their edges start to soften. This takes varying time depending on the type of potato. Sweet potatoes cook extremely quickly. New Potatoes should never be roasted in my view – too good boiled!

4) Once the potatoes have soft edges but are still hard in their middles, they are ready to drain. Once drained, place the lid back on the saucepan and shake the pan vigorously. This knocks away the soft edges of the potatoes and makes them fluffy. Now leave on the side with the lid OFF. They get fluffier as they cool off a bit and more water evaporates off them.

5) Prepare the roasting tin or dish. Place the oil in with salt and pepper. Pop in the oven and heat up for around 5–8 minutes.

6) Once the oil is really hot, tip the potatoes into it (they should sizzle), moving them about so they become coated in the oil. Sprinkle the herbs over and place back in oven.

7) Cook for 25 minutes, then turn the potatoes over and continue cooking until they are an amazing golden brown colour. Use a slotted spoon to lift out and serve red hot.

Tip: Best served with rich gravy, although my mayo is also a great accompaniment. Make sure you make enough potatoes!

Tip: Try adding finely diced garlic and a sprinkle of smoked paprika around the last twenty minutes of roasting.

GRAVY

Basic Gravy

¼ pint / 150ml Vegetable Stock (use your own home made one for great results – see Skill Set section)

1 tablespoon Reduced Salt Soya Sauce

¼ –½ tablespoon Tomato Purée (depending on how tomato based your stock already is)

½ teaspoon Sugar

1 heaped teaspoon Cornflour

¼ teaspoon Marmite (you won't taste this – it is merely a seasoning)

½ teaspoon Sherry or Red Wine Vinegar (or similar)

1 tablespoon Non-Dairy Margarine

1) Place the cornflour in a saucepan and add the veg stock gradually to avoid clumping, stirring all the while.

2) Add the other ingredients.

3) Bring gradually to the boil, stirring continually.

4) Once the gravy has thickened, taste it and if it needs pepper or salt, add this now.

Tip: You can make the gravy before it is needed and re-heat. It becomes slightly thicker this way too.

Tip: If you find the gravy too rich, then take out half, add water and another teaspoon of cornflour and bring back to the boil, stirring all the time. Keep the other half for another day.

Extra Rich Gravy

250ml Vegetable Stock

1 tablespoon Non-Dairy Margarine

1 teaspoon dried Mixed Herbs

1 tablespoon Dark Soya Sauce

2 halves Sun-dried Tomatoes

1 tablespoon Red Wine or 1 teaspoon Sherry Vinegar

6 ready-cooked Sweet Chestnuts

Salt & Pepper

1 teaspoon Paprika

½ tablespoon Cornflour mixed in a little water

Optional 10 Blackberries if you have them

Take all of the ingredients and whiz together in a blender or processor. Heat slowly, stirring continually until it comes to the boil. Then simmer for a few minutes. Taste and add further seasonings if you wish. Again, if too rich for your palate, remove a third to use another day and add water to the remainder. You may need to add more cornflour too to thicken, remembering to always add cornflour in a little of its own water first.

Gravy without a Vegetable Stock

6–8 Cooked Sweet Chestnuts
1 Sun-dried Tomato (in or out of oil)
1 tablespoon Non-Dairy margarine
½ teaspoon Marmite
1 teaspoon Agave or Soft Brown Sugar
½ teaspoon Cyder vinegar

1 tablespoon red wine (optional)
1 tablespoon Cornflour
¼ teaspoon Garlic Salt
½ teaspoon Paprika
Pepper
Enough water to make ½ pint

Place everything into a small blender or hand blend in a bowl until the chestnuts and tomato are completely smooth. Then put the liquid into a saucepan and heat, stirring all the while, and bring to the boil. It will thicken and darken in colour. If you want it thicker still, take another teaspoon of cornflour and mix in a cup with a little cold water then add it to the gravy, stirring as you do so.

Cheating at Gravy

For those days when you can't actually be bothered to make a gravy from scratch, just boost an instant vegetable gravy with onions fried in butter and a drop of wine. Simmer the lot in a pan for a few minutes.

Also make an instant gravy using boiling veg stock from the pan of veg you are cooking.

SWEET CHESTNUT PATÉ

SWEET CHESTNUT PATÉ

Time: Prep and blitz takes around 15 minutes. Makes approx. 600ml paté

1½ cups plain Cashews
15–18 cooked Sweet Chestnuts
4–6 Sun-dried Tomato halves
Pepper
1 Lemon juiced

1 tablespoon light Soya Sauce
6–8 leaves of fresh Rosemary
6–8 tips of fresh Basil
8–10 Chives
4–6 tablespoons Non-Dairy Single Cream

This is about finding the texture and flavour for you, hence the 'round-about' amounts of ingredients. Simply take everything here and place into a food processor and blitz. Keep stopping and scraping down the sides of the bowl. Make sure you add enough juice and cream to help the processor turn, as this is a very thick paste. I tend to use the 'pulse' button quite a lot to start. Don't over blitz as the texture and colour is wonderful.

PATÉ, SPREADS & SAUCES

FIG & CHESTNUT PATÉ

Time: around 15 minutes to prep and blitz. Makes approx. 600 ml paté

1 cup plain Cashews
8–10 cooked Sweet Chestnuts
4–6 pre-cooked Figs
2–4 Sun-dried Tomato Halves
Pepper
Salt
1 Lime juiced

1 small clove Garlic
3–4 tablespoons Non-Dairy Single Cream
2 teaspoons oil
½ teaspoon Cyder Vinegar
5 Chives
½ teaspoon Allspice (this is *not* the same as Ground Mixed Spice)

This paté has a spicy fruity punch, like a fruit pickle or chutney. It makes a really good change from the other patés here.

Simply place everything into a food processor and blitz to the desired texture. Make sure there is enough liquid for the processor to be able to turn as the paste is very thick. Cream and oil are good to soften, although a little water can be used if necessary. Little by little is the key; keep tasting as you go.

Tip: This makes a great filling for peppers, with couscous or rice added to the mix.

FIG & CHESTNUT PATÉ

PECAN, APPLE & RED WINE PATÉ

PECAN, APPLE & RED WINE PATÉ (BAKED)

Time: 15 mins prep, 30 mins baking. Oven 170°C. Makes approx. 600ml

1 cup Pecans
½ Bramley Apple (cooking apple)
2–3 halves Sun-dried Tomatoes
6–8 soft Prunes
2 tablespoons good Red Wine
1 tablespoon Non-Dairy Margarine

2 tablespoons Non-Dairy Cream
½ teaspoon dried Mixed Herbs
Fresh Ground Pepper
1 slice Brown / Granary Bread
Pinch Garlic Salt
6 leaves fresh Rosemary

1) Place nuts, apple (peeled, cored and diced), tomatoes, prunes and red wine into a food processor and blitz for 1 minute.

2) Add the bread, Rosemary, garlic salt, herbs and pepper and blitz another minute.

3) Add remaining margarine and cream and blitz until a smoothish consistency. You will need to keep spooning down the sides of the bowl, and possibly help the paté to thoroughly mix at first. It is ready when it begins to ball and travel around the bowl on its own. If this is just not happening add a little more liquid – milk is good for this, a drop at a time.

4) Place into a shallow oven-proof dish (small size), smooth down and place on middle shelf for 30 minutes in a pre-heated oven.

5) Alternatively keep it raw and chill.

For best results allow to cool completely then chill before eating. This is a wonderfully rich paté that rivals anything on the market in my opinion.

ALMOND, CHESTNUT & RED WINE PATÉ

Time: 15 minutes prep, and 30 minutes chill time

- 1 cup Blanched Almonds (without their brown skins)
- 12 cooked Sweet Chestnuts
- ½ Lime juiced
- ½ tablespoon Dark Soya Sauce
- 2 halves Sun-dried Tomatoes
- 8 Chives
- Few fresh Rosemary leaves
- 1 tablespoon Non-Dairy Margarine
- 3 tablespoons Non-Dairy Single Cream
- 2 tablespoons Red Cooking Wine

Place the almonds into a food processor and blitz to break them up a bit. Then add the rest of the ingredients and blitz until you have the texture you desire.

If you only have unblanched almonds, these can be used but there will be a slight 'grittiness' in the texture. You can easily remove the skins by soaking the almonds in water over-night. They then slip off relatively easily.

SMOKED TOASTED ALMOND & CHILLI PATÉ (BAKED)

This has an extraordinary flavour and texture when placed in a sandwich with my mayonnaise. My son reckons it tastes better than a BBQ Chicken Sandwich, and they were one of his favourites! It has a great fiery colour this paté too, which gives it a real Mexican look.

Time: 15 mins prep, 40 minutes baking. Oven 170°C. Makes approx. 600ml

- 1 cup Toasted Whole Almonds (blanched)
- 4–6 Ready Cooked Sweet Chestnuts
- 2–3 halves Sun-dried Tomatoes
- ½ Bell Pepper
- 1 slice Wholemeal Bread
- ½ Lemon / Lime juiced
- 6–8 leaves fresh Rosemary
- ¼ teaspoon Garlic Salt
- ¼ teaspoon Smoked Paprika (smoked is optional)
- ½ teaspoon Mild Chilli Powder
- 1 tablespoon Non-Dairy Margarine
- 2 tablespoons Non-Dairy Cream
- 1 tablespoon Dark Soya Sauce
- ½ tablespoon Red Wine Vinegar

1) Take the almonds, chestnuts, tomatoes, bell pepper (roughly diced) and bread and place in a food processor and blitz for 1 minute.

2) Add the rest of the ingredients and blitz until reasonably smooth in texture.

3) Place the mixture into a small oven-proof dish, smooth down and bake on the middle shelf in a pre-heated oven for 40 minutes. For best results allow to cool thoroughly then chill before eating.

Tip: This is a rich, spicy and aromatic paté which can be mixed with other paté or mayo in bread, with pasta, on crackers, with raw vegetables – any way you want. And is great for stuffing mini peppers, courgettes or small aubergines.

PATÉ NUGGETS

Great for buffets, picnics and a light lunch. Can also use my Nut Roast to make these too, mixed with a little paté and tomato sauce.

Time: So quick! 20 mins chill time. As long as you have the paté already made. Makes enough for two

140g / 4–6 heaped tablespoons Paté (any of those in the book)
2 large White Potatoes, peeled & diced
Handful Young Leaf Spinach, chopped
Handful of fresh Basil leaves, chopped
2 halves Sun-dried Tomatoes, diced
1 slice Wholemeal Bread, crumbed

1 tablespoon Non-Dairy Margarine
1 tablespoon Red Wine
1 teaspoon Sugar (optional)
1 teaspoon Paprika
Zest of ½ Lemon / Lime
Little flour
Some vegetable oil for frying

1) Cook potato – peal and cube small, cook until tender and drain. Place into a mixing bowl and allow to cool enough to handle with your fingers.

2) Coarsely chop the Basil, Spinach and finely dice the tomatoes. Add to the bowl

3) Crumb the bread and add to the bowl along with all the other ingredients. The paté can be added and broken up with your fingers.

4) Now using your hands mix all of the ingredients together.

5) Sprinkle flour on the work surface, take a small handful of mixture and form into a sausage shape. Place on a plate and once all the mixture has been made into sausage shapes, chill for 20 minutes.

6) Now using a sharp knife, cut the sausages into 'coins' and place into hot oil in a frying pan. Don't use too much oil and make sure it is really hot so the coins do not soak too much of it up. Keep the coins small, no bigger than a ten pence piece in diameter for the best results.

7) Once the coins are crisp each side, lift them out and place on some kitchen towel to drain excess oil from them. These are lovely with ketchup or mayo and good even when cold. Good in a sandwich too!

PATÉ NUGGETS

HUMMUS

Time: 10 minutes plus chill time. Makes approx. 400ml

- 350ml pack / tin cooked Chickpeas, drained (keep some of the juice)
- 1 clove Garlic
- Juice of 1 Lemon
- 1 tablespoon Cashew Butter (in place of Tahini)
- 1 tablespoon Olive Oil (optional)
- Pinch Coarse Salt
- ½ tablespoon Ground Cumin
- Enough Chickpea juice to create desired thickness and texture

Place everything into a food processor and blitz until smooth. Can be blitzed to any texture you like and you can add any quantity of juice to create the perfect personal thickness or silkiness.

Chill in an air-tight container for up to 7 days.

CHILLI & TURMERIC HUMMUS

CHILLI & TURMERIC HUMMUS

Time: 10 minutes plus chill time. Makes approx. 400ml

350ml pack of pre-cooked Chickpeas, drained (keep some of the juice)

1 clove Garlic

Juice of 1 Lemon or Lime

2 halves of Sun-dried Tomato in oil

Pinch Coarse Salt

1 teaspoon Turmeric

1 teaspoon Mild Chilli Powder

Two pinches dried crushed Chillies

1 teaspoon Ground Cumin or Garam Masala

Enough Chickpea Juice to create desired texture and thickness.

Blitz everything in a food processor adding chickpea juice to form the texture and thickness you like. Chill in an air-tight container for up to 7 days.

PATÉ, SPREADS & SAUCES

MAYONNAISE

Time: 10 minutes Makes approx. 400ml

- 360g Firm Silken Tofu (no need to press this)
- ½ Lemon or Lime juiced
- 3 teaspoons Cyder Vinegar
- 3 tablespoons Oil
- ¼ teaspoon Garlic Salt
- ¼ teaspoon ground Coriander
- Finely ground Black pepper
- Spot of Mustard
- Pinch of salt
- 1 tablespoon Caster / Soft Brown Sugar

Simply put all of the ingredients into a blender and whiz until smooth. Taste and add as you go. You can add dried herbs, pepper and salt if you wish. Chives are good too and some fresh Basil.

This mayonnaise is used in the following recipes; Potato Salad, Pasta Salad and Coleslaw.

MAYONNAISE

COLESLAW

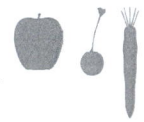

Time: Quick if you have the mayo already made, makes approx. 800ml

Centre of a Green Cabbage, or one small White Cabbage

2 large Carrots

2 medium Onions

Optional addition of Radishes, Celery, Apple, Walnuts, etc.

3–6 tablespoons of Mayonnaise, depending on how creamy you want it.

1) Very finely slice the ingredients and place in a large bowl and toss together with fingers.

2) Add the mayonnaise and with a spoon, thoroughly mix it all together to evenly distribute. If the mayo is too thick, add a little cream or olive oil to it.

You could grind fresh pepper on top or some chopped chives for presentation. This is actually a very attractive side dish if placed carefully into a decorated bowl.

POTATO SALAD

Time: As quick as cooking new potatoes that are cut very small. Will need mayo already made

Two tablespoons Mayonnaise
1 teaspoon mixed Herbs, dried or fresh

Squeeze of Lemon or Lime
New Potatoes – around 10–12

1) Chop the potatoes up into small cubes, keeping the skins on.

2) Rinse and place in a pan of fresh water, so the potatoes are just covered and sprinkle a generous pinch of sea salt. Bring potatoes to the boil and then simmer until tender.

3) Drain potatoes and transfer to a bowl and add all the other ingredients. Stir well so all of the potatoes get smothered adding more mayo if required.

4) This salad can be eaten warm or chilled before serving – if chilling the dressing will thicken rather like cream cheese, so it would be a good idea to add more oil to the mayo before adding it to the potatoes. Sprinkle with freshly ground pepper and a little Paprika for colour.

POTATO SALAD

CUCUMBER, MINT & LEMON RAITA

Time: Prep only minutes, then chill

200ml Plain Soya Yoghurt (or you may like to try this with Coconut or Almond Yoghurt) even better if strained to thicken

Salt & Pepper

¼ Cucumber, seeded and diced

Couple of sprigs of Mint

1 Lemon juiced and zested (or Lime)

Ground pepper

1) Cut the cucumber all the way down the middle lengthways and scoop out the wet pulpy seed part and discard.

2) Chop the cucumber up very small so that it is delicate and light when mixed with the yoghurt later. Place it in a small mixing bowl.

3) Chop the mint very finely and add to the cucumber along with the zest and the lemon juice. Add a generous pinch of sea salt.

4) Grind a little pepper and leave in the fridge for the yoghurt to become infused with the flavours.

5) When you serve, mix up again and transfer to a fresh bowl and decorate with a sprig of mint or similar and some lemon zest.

Tip: Chill for as long as you can as it gets better with time as flavours infuse the yoghurt.

Tip: Try alternatives such as using Coriander and tomato, or spring onion and sweet corn. You really can use anything at all.

Tip: Another great side dish with a hot curry or spicy dish is simply banana sliced and added to plain yoghurt. It has an amazing cooling effect on the mouth.

'CHEESY' CREAM SAUCE

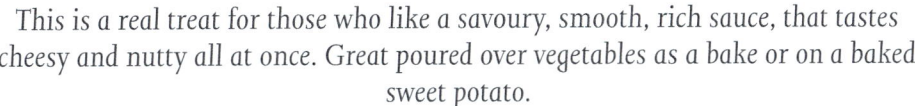

This is a real treat for those who like a savoury, smooth, rich sauce, that tastes cheesy and nutty all at once. Great poured over vegetables as a bake or on a baked sweet potato.

Time: 10 minutes. Makes approx. 500ml

- 300ml Nut Milk (Cashew or Almond works best I find, and home-made is amazing! See the Skills Set section 'Making Nut Milk', page 28)
- 150ml Non-Dairy Cream or plain yoghurt
- Generous salt and pepper seasoning
- 3–4 tablespoons Nutritional Yeast
- 1½ tablespoons Cornflour
- 1 tablespoon Non-Dairy margarine
- ¼ teaspoon or less of Mustard (not the powder but the ready-made)
- For an extra taste add a handful of diced Chives

So easy it takes a moment.

Put all of the ingredients into a saucepan and with a hand whisk (or fork to begin then a spoon) stir as you gently heat the mixture to boiling point. Do this slowly or lumps will form.

Once boiling, simmer gently for a couple of minutes to fully thicken, stirring continually. If too thick add a little more milk and stir in.

PATÉ, SPREADS & SAUCES

BASIL CREAM PASTA SAUCE

A quick and deliciously fresh sauce, with an amazing pale green colour. Only use fresh Basil and Parsley.

- Lots of fresh Basil....as much as you can handle!
- A touch of Flat Leaf Parsley
- 1 cup of Non-Dairy Single Cream
- 1 tablespoon light vegetable oil (optional)
- 1–2 teaspoons Lemon Juice
- 1–2 tablespoons White Wine
- Salt and Pepper to taste
- 1 teaspoon of cornflour in a little water added if you want to heat the sauce and thicken it.
- Anything else you might like to add – I like a couple of pinches of freshly ground Coriander and sometimes a touch of dried Tarragon, especially if the sauce is heated.

Blitz the lot in a small blender jug / use hand blender or processor and use cold or warm up to go with anything you like. Great with pasta and mushrooms, grilled tomatoes and bread. Just go with your taste buds.

PASTA SALAD

This can mean many things. To some it is a tomato sauce-based cold salad containing pasta, or a creamy mayo salad containing pasta, warm or cold. Here I am doing both, creaming together some tomato paste with the mayo and keeping it warm.

Time: Pasta cooking time depends on what you use

Some Pasta shapes
Some Mayonnaise
1–2 teaspoons Tomato Purée
Generous grinding of Pepper
Lime Juice and zest

Tablespoon honey substitute
1 tablespoon Olive Oil
Finely chopped Tomatoes, Radishes, Carrots, Spring Onions and Bell Peppers
Optional additional of chilli powder or ground dried chillies

1) Cook the pasta.

2) Whilst pasta is cooking take all the vegetables and chop finely and place into a mixing bowl. The amounts of each will depend of how much pasta you are cooking. Chop everything smaller than the pasta.

3) When pasta is cooked, drain and add to the bowl of other ingredients. Stir thoroughly.

4) Put all the sauce ingredients into a bowl or blender and whiz together, so they combine well. Warm the sauce if you wish or serve it cold. Drizzle over the pasta and vegetables and serve.

This is so much about personal taste and I change mine every time I do it, so I can't really give you definite measurements. It will taste interesting whatever you do and it is good practise to use your taste-buds to determine amounts of ingredients and their combination.

SARAH'S BOMBAY POTATOES

These are lovely with yoghurt, sprinkled with fresh coriander and bread. Great as a side dish to anything, and great made with unpeeled new potatoes.

Time: 30–40 minutes

White or Sweet Potatoes, diced bite-size and precooked, drained. Can be chilled until needed.

1 Onion, diced

2 Garlic cloves, diced

2 tablespoons Non-Dairy Margarine

1 tablespoon Raw Coconut Oil (if you have it)

Salt and Pepper

½ tablespoon Mild or Medium Curry Powder

1 teaspoon Garam Masala

2 tablespoons Tomato Purée

Juice of one Lemon or Lime

Couple of tablespoons of water

Fresh Coriander and Non-Dairy Plain Yoghurt optional to serve

1) Pre-cook and drain the potatoes. Place to the side with the lid removed.

2) In a saucepan, melt the margarine (and coconut oil) and add the onions and garlic, diced or sliced as you like. Gently sizzle until they begin to brown.

3) Add the spices and allow to sizzle for 2–3 minutes, stirring now and then.

4) Add tomato Purée, water and lemon/lime juice and stir thoroughly. Add salt and pepper.

5) Now add the cooked potatoes and stir carefully so as not to break up the potatoes too much. Once all mixed and covered in the spiced sauce, keep on the lowest heat to warm through (You could do this in a covered oven-proof dish in the oven, on a low heat). As the potatoes warm up, stir them occasionally and add more water if it looks as if it might be sticking to the pan or burning. You want to produce a thick, starchy sauce around the potatoes.

6) Serve when heated through thoroughly.

Tip: Nice served with strained yoghurt flavoured with mint, see Raita (page 94).

GRILLED COURGETTES

Great on their own on toast or as a side with other things. Surprisingly tasty and juicy.

Time: 10–12 minutes

2 medium Courgettes thinly sliced lengthwise with skins on

1 tablespoon Olive Oil

Sprinkling of Pepper, Garlic Salt, Cajun Spice, dried Tarragon, Soft Brown Sugar

Juice of ½ Lemon

Agave Nectar or Maple Syrup for serving

1) Wash the courgettes. Slice them lengthwise as thinly as you can but not so that they are translucent. It is better if they have a little depth to them as they shrink on cooking.

2) Place some foil on a baking tray and lay out the courgettes close together. Brush or drizzle on the olive oil.

3) Sprinkle on the seasonings taking care not to overdo them. Less is more since courgettes are subtle in flavour.

4) Sprinkle with the lemon juice and place under a medium to hot grill, for around 6–8 minutes.

5) Take a look at the courgettes. They are ready when they start to form brown and golden spots on them. This is the sugars caramelising.

6) No need to turn the courgettes over. This way they keep their juiciness. When dishing out, don't waste the juice in the baking tray – it is the best bit! Drizzle on some syrup if you like the extra sweetness and a little salt.

PATÉ, SPREADS & SAUCES

SMOKED PAPRIKA CHIPS

SMOKED PAPRIKA CHIPS

A lovely sweet smoked twist to the humble home-made chip

Time: 20–30 minutes

Firm White Potatoes peeled
Oil to shallow fry
Salt, Pepper

Smoked paprika
Optional mixed dried Herbs
1 Lemon

1) Peel and slice potatoes into chips no thicker than your little finger, making the chips as equal in size as you can. This is so they all cook equally.

2) Place the raw chips in a sauce pan and cover with cold water and bring to the boil. Once boiling, remove from heat drain and run under cold water. Then shake off excess water in a colander.

3) Heat oil in a pan, just enough so the oil covers the whole bottom of the pan.

4) Test the heat of the oil by adding one chip. It needs to sizzle and bubble and when it does the oil is ready. Add the chips and spread out. You may find they don't all touch the oil but that doesn't matter as you will be moving them as they cook.

5) Sprinkle seasoning and using a tea strainer, sprinkle the smoked paprika generously over the chips. This will only need to be done once as it is quite a strong spice.

6) Let the chips sizzle for 3–4 minutes then using a spatula or fish slice, turn and move the chips around, making sure that the most raw ones get to touch the oil.

7) Keep the chips sizzling and moving until they are all golden in colour.

8) With a slotted spoon or similar, remove the chips from the oil and place in a colander that has been lined with kitchen paper to remove excess oil

Tip: Serve immediately with a slice of lemon which can be used in place of vinegar as it accompanies the smoked paprika really well. Best chips ever! Great with grilled tomatoes, mushrooms and fried cabbage.

ONION SIDE SALAD

ONION SIDE SALAD

Onions are surprisingly refreshing when prepared this way as the vinegar and sugar neutralise the sting of the milk in the onion. Good side dish with spicy food or with richly flavoured bread and potato salad.

Time: 20–30 minutes

2 strong White Onions, finely diced
1 Red Apple, diced
¼ Cucumber, finely diced
4 Radishes, diced
Handful of Mixed Dried Fruit

Salt & Pepper
2 tablespoons Cyder Vinegar
½ Lemon, juiced
2 tablespoons caster Sugar or sweetener such as Agave

1) Peel and slice onions so they are thin but not too small. Translucent strips is what I aim for.

2) Place onion in a bowl and separate the layers with your fingers. Place the vinegar, lemon and sugar, salt and pepper into the bowl and mix thoroughly.

3) Now cut open the apple and core it, but leave the skin on. Slice then dice the flesh very small. The idea is to make the salad look very delicate, so each ingredient is made small and precise. Add the apple to the bowl and stir well. The vinegar and lemon juice will prevent the apple going brown.

4) Slice the cucumber lengthways and scoop out the seeds with a teaspoon. Discard these. Now slice and dice the firm flesh and add to the bowl.

5) Add dried fruit and sliced radishes, again nice and finely chopped.

6) Stir everything together, cover and pop in the fridge for 20 minutes to allow the onions to sweeten.

Tip: Try using different sorts of onions such as red, spring and shallots.

STIR-FRY SAUCES

Stir-fries do not require a wok or any specialist knowledge about foreign food. They are very nutritious because the vegetables are cooked very quickly and they keep their crunch and sweetness.

You can buy many ready-made sauces now, some of which are vegan, but it is good to have some idea how to put one together yourself. So here are three of my quick and useful stir-fry sauces that go with anything at all. These sauces go a long way, but easily coat enough vegetables and noodles for 3–4 adults. What you don't use can be kept in the fridge.

Sweet Spiced

2 tablespoons Tomato Ketchup

½ teaspoon Mustard (English)

1 teaspoon sugar or honey substitute

½ Lemon or Lime juiced plus zest

¼ tsp Garam Masala curry mix

Seasoning

Just add all of this together, mix well and refrigerate until required.

Garlic & Ginger

1 cm fresh Ginger peeled and blitzed with one small clove Garlic

2 tablespoons Tomato Ketchup

A glug of Olive Oil (or similar)

A glug of Light Soya Sauce

Salt & Pepper

Orange juice (optional to loosen the sauce)

Blitz this all together in a small blender, or chop finely and mix by hand.

Peanut & Ginger – makes 1½ cups of sauce

1 small Onion

1 small clove Garlic

1 inch fresh Ginger

½ Lemon or Lime juiced

2 tablespoons oil

6 tablespoons Soya cream

1 tablespoon Peanut Butter (or Cashew Butter)

1 tablespoon Light Soya Sauce

4 tablespoons Water

Touch chilli powder and Seasoning

In the oil, gently fry the finely chopped onion, garlic and ginger until soft and sweet…add the lemon/lime juice.

Add this to a blender with all of the other ingredients and blitz until smooth.

Refrigerate until required.

Sweet Ginger & Lemon – makes 1¼ cups

1 cup water
1 cm fresh Ginger diced
1 small clove garlic diced
2 tablespoons Dark Soya Sauce
½ lemon juiced
1½ tablespoon Agave Nectar
¼ teaspoon Salt
¼ teaspoon Garlic Salt
1 teaspoon ground ginger
2 tablespoons veg or nut oil
1 teaspoon rice wine vinegar
½ tablespoon cornflour

Simply place everything into a small food processor and blend together until smooth.

Chill until required.

All of these sauces can be altered with small amounts of spice, chives, spring onions and chillies. Just try things out for yourself and see what suits. Also take a look at the ingredients on the back of pre-made sauces to get an idea of what is in them then try your own version.

Tip: Try adding a small amount of mixed dried fruit or apple, mango or pineapple to your stir-fries.

MAIN SALADS

There is no recipe for a salad, in my humble opinion. The permutations are endless, and recipes can stop us experimenting and keeping our interest fed. What is probably most helpful is a couple of pointers.

1) Forget lettuce, cucumber and tomato as the salad of British choice. It lacks everything that makes salad great – imagination!

2) Think COLOUR, TEXTURE, FLAVOUR, and FRESH.

3) When in your supermarket or grocers, be imaginative and throw caution to the wind. Fruit is great in a salad, whether it be a pink grapefruit or a nectarine, put a little in a crunchy salad and it lifts it. It is a natural zing and sweetness.

4) Nuts and seeds add a different crunch and flavour.

5) Lettuce is great when it has some colour and crinkle – try something new, and don't forget cabbage is great in salad as long as it is cut finely so you are not chomping on it for hours.

6) Fresh herbs come into their own. Try one or two, little to start and see how they work. With a vinaigrette dressing you will find your mouth waking up and being tantalised by fresh flavour and re-vitalising goodness.

7) Sometimes I like to toast nuts and eat them while they are still warm, tossed into the salad. Small cubes of potato or sautéed mushrooms are good like this too.

8) Have fun and get the kids involved. Making salad is really an edible art and craft session – get creative!

SALAD WITH APPLE, PECANS AND CREAM DRESSING

DRESSINGS

Salads can be taken from the position of 'good' to 'amazing!' by a good dressing. I try not to use oil in mine as this carries with it many calories, and also makes the salad slimy if kept longer than a day.

Take the ingredients of the dressings offered here and experiment yourself with additions and combinations. Fresh mint it wonderful and so is fresh basil.

The mayonnaise recipe makes a good dressing if it is thinned down with wine or vinegar or juice. Again, try things and keep tasting.

Nan's Simple Dressing

Once the salad is made, sprinkle a teaspoon of caster sugar over it, followed by juice of half a lemon or lime, and a teaspoon of Cyder vinegar. Toss the salad and leave at room temperature for 30 minutes or so. Nanny Dell would have loved this one!

Mustard Vinaigrette

Mix in a cup, one teaspoon vinegar (avoid malt), and one teaspoon agave nectar or maple syrup, juice of half a lemon, grind of fresh pepper, pinch of salt and a pinch (or more) of mustard. Whisk with a fork and drizzle over the salad before serving.

Herb Vinaigrette

In a cup, half a tablespoon white wine, one teaspoon agave nectar, salt and pepper, juice of half a lemon and a teaspoon of mixed herbs. Whisk with a fork and drizzle over salad before serving. To make it creamier whisk a little non-dairy cream into it.

Cream Dressing

Into a bowl add 1 tablespoon tofu (or cream), juice of half a lemon or lime, teaspoon of vinegar, salt, pepper and half teaspoon of dried Tarragon. Whisk with a hand whisk or blender until creamy and smooth and drizzle over salad.

Alternatively, take a tablespoon of mayonnaise and add the rest. The mayonnaise recipe in this book is very good on salad.

MAIN DISHES...

Curries, pies, stews, pasta and rice dishes.

COTTAGE PIE

CLASSIC RATATOUILLE

CLASSIC RATATOUILLE

Time: 20 minutes prep, 20 minutes cooking. Serves 4–6

- 3–5 tablespoons Olive Oil
- 3 large Onions, sliced
- 6 cloves Garlic, roughly diced
- 6–8 large Bell Peppers of various colours, roughly chopped
- 6 small Courgettes, roughly chopped
- 6–8 ripe Plum Tomatoes, diced
- Bay leaf
- 1 tablespoon dried Herbs (of Provence mix)
- ½ teaspoon Salt
- Freshly ground pepper
- 200g Passata or more if you wish
- 3–4 tablespoons good White Wine
- Squeeze of Lemon – optional
- (You can add aubergine but I don't like it! I sometimes add some cauliflower or broccoli)
- 1–2 tablespoons Non-Dairy Margarine (optional to make the sauce gleam)
- Fresh Basil is great torn and thrown on top when served.

I once read that the secret to good Ratatouille is cooking each item in the right order. Not sure about this, but I tend to start with the onions and garlic then add in the order I have listed the ingredients, cooking for 4 minutes with each new ingredient.

1) In a large lidded saucepan, sauté the onion and garlic in the oil until the onions start to brown. Then add the peppers, stir thoroughly and cook for 4 minutes gently with the lid on.

2) Add the courgettes and again stir thoroughly and cook for 4 minutes with the lid on.

3) Add tomatoes……as above

4) Add aubergines if using……as above

5) Add all the herbs and seasonings and the passata… as above.

6) Lastly add the wine and the lemon juice.

7) Taste the ratatouille to see if you require more salt, pepper or herbs, then turn off heat and leave in the pan with the lid on until you wish to eat it. If this is not on the same day, then cool, and keep refrigerated in an air tight container. It also freezes well.

Tip. When you wish to eat it, re-heat thoroughly. The flavours deepen on re-heating and always taste better the next day.

Check out the Mediterranean Stew which is based upon this Ratatouille dish, but is made richer.

MAIN DISHES

CHILLI

Good with rice and yoghurt but also just as great on a jacket potato, with chips or in a wrap.

Time: 30 minutes. Feeds 4

- ½ cup / tin Haricot Beans (well drained)
- ½ cup / tin Black Beans (well drained)
- 2 ripe Plum Tomatoes
- 1 can chopped Tomatoes
- 1 Bell Pepper, diced
- 2 Red Onions, diced
- 3 cloves Garlic, finely diced
- 1 small Courgette, diced
- Salt & pepper
- 1 teaspoon dried Thyme
- ½ tablespoon mild or hot Chilli Powder
- 2 pinches of dried crushed Chillies
- 1 tablespoon Paprika (or hot paprika if you have it)
- ½ teaspoon Allspice (optional)
- ½ tablespoon Red Wine Vinegar (or cooking red wine)
- 2 tablespoons good Olive Oil
- 2 tablespoons Nutritional Yeast (optional)
- Optional cornflour as thickener

1) Prepare all the vegetables by chopping quite small. Warm the olive oil and sizzle the onions and garlic.

2) Add the seasonings and spices and allow to sizzle for a few minutes so the oil in the powders are released.

3) Add the plum tomatoes (chopped) and stir in. Add the tinned tomatoes and the wine vinegar.

4) Add the courgette to the pan along with the yeast and pepper and stir well. At this point add the beans, drained of any of their liquid.

5) Bring to the boil then turn down the heat, place the lid on the pan and simmer gently for 10 minutes.

6) To thicken the sauce further remove the pan lid and simmer for another 5 minutes or add some cornflour (a teaspoon at a time in a little of its own water).

GENTLE FUSION DAL

I am a great believer in using up left-overs and often make extra Ratatouille so that I can make this Dal the next day.

Time: 1 hour to soak lentils, then cooking time for lentils chosen

300–500ml / 1–2 cups leftover Ratatouille*

1 cup of rinsed and soaked Red Lentils (or other of your choice)

1 tablespoon Raw Coconut Oil

½ Lemon / Lime juiced

½ tablespoon Soft Brown Sugar

1½ teaspoons Mild or Medium Curry Powder (or a mix)

½–1 teaspoon Paprika

2–3 tablespoons Soya Plain Yoghurt or Cream

Salt to taste

Possibly extra Tomato Purée if using smaller amount of Ratatouille

1) Place coconut oil into a large saucepan with a lid. Melt gently, then add the spices and allow to come to a sizzle.

2) Add the drained lentils, and lemon juice and stir thoroughly.

3) Now add enough water to cover the lentils and bring to the boil. Boil rapidly for five-10 minutes, then bring down to a low simmer. Do all of this with the lid on.

4) Add the Ratatouille and sugar, stir thoroughly and add further water if the lentils require it.

5) Bring back to a gentle simmer until the lentils are fully cooked and soft. Time for this will vary according to the lentil you use. Red lentils cook quickest. Taste it and add salt if required.

6) Finally turn off the heat, add the yoghurt, stir then hand blend a little to thicken, but not entirely so that there is some texture and colour variance.

Great served with bread.

* If you have no Ratatouille, then before making the dal, simply fry in 2 tablespoons margarine: (roughly sliced) 2 onions, 2 garlic cloves, 2 bell peppers, 2 courgettes, 2 plum tomatoes, 2 tbsp tomato Purée and some dried herbs, with ½ cup water. Simmer until partly tender, so around 10–12 minutes. Then use this to add to the Dal at stage 4.

BUTTON MUSHROOMS IN SWEET CHESTNUT SAUCE

Time: Sauce takes 15 minutes, putting together the dish takes 10 minutes. Serves 2

BUTTON MUSHROOMS IN SWEET CHESTNUT SAUCE

Small Button White or Chestnut Mushrooms (250–300g), rinsed but left whole.

6–8 Sweet Cooked Chestnuts
½ teaspoon Lemon Juice
80–100ml / ⅓ cup Non-Dairy Single Cream
80–100ml / ⅓ cup Water
½ teaspoon Cornflour
½–1 tablespoon Non-Dairy Margarine

Non-Dairy Margarine

Sauce:

Salt
Leaves of Rosemary from one inch of stem
4–6 Chives or ¼ teaspoon Garlic Salt
1 tablespoon White Wine

1) Make the sauce first as this can be chilled and used whenever you like. Put all the sauce ingredients into a small blender/processor and blitz to smooth and creamy. Taste and adjust to your liking.

2) When ready to prepare the meal, the mushrooms simply need gently cooking in melted margarine for around 5–7 minutes until tender. Whilst they are cooking you can heat the sauce in a pan gradually, stirring continually. It will thicken as it approaches boiling point. At this time, turn the heat down a little and stir as it cooks for around 3–4 minutes until the cornflour can no longer be felt on the tongue.

Tip: This dish goes well with pasta, crispy chips, a jacket potato or salad and bread.

Tip: Take care with fresh rosemary. It is very pungent and in a delicate sauce like this can overpower it very easily.

Tip: As an alternative to rosemary, try tarragon, or some lemon.

BAKED BEAN & NEW POTATO PIE

Time: 30 minutes prep, 40–45 minutes bake. Oven 190°C

BAKED BEAN & NEW POTATO PIE

Pastry

250g / 10 oz Plain Flour

75g / 3 oz Vegetable Suet

50g / 2 oz Non-Dairy Margarine

Generous pinch of Salt (up to ¼ teaspoon)

5–6 tablespoons cold Water

Filling

400–500g Jersey Royal New Potatoes, skins left on and cut into bite size pieces.

415g tin Baked Beans

Salt & Pepper

2 tablespoons Soya Sauce

Optional dried herbs

Optional Sun-dried Tomatoes

1) Cut the potatoes into small pieces and rinse thoroughly. Place in a saucepan and cover with water. Add generous pinch of salt and bring to the boil. Cook until tender, and drain thoroughly.

2) Whilst the potatoes are cooking prepare the pastry. Place flour and a generous pinch of salt into a mixing bowl. Add the two fats and mix with the flour using your finger-tips, producing a breadcrumb texture.

3) Add the water and with your fingers mix with the dry ingredients, Begin to squeeze the mix together to form a ball. If it seems to keep falling apart, break up and add a touch more water then try again. This is quite a dry feeling pastry, so don't add too much water.

4) Take two-thirds of the dough ball and squeeze into a small, thick disc shape in your hands. Place on a floured surface. Roll it carefully, turning after every single roll front and back again. Don't roll right up over the edges or it starts to split apart.

5) Once the pastry is rolled large enough to cover the base and the sides of the tin, stop, and grease the tin with some margarine. Place the pastry carefully in and with a bent forefinger, press it into the corner allowing the extra pastry to sit over the edge – don't cut it off yet. If it splits or you jab a hole into it, don't worry. This pastry is like play dough – you can patch up and press together and it all just mends itself when it cooks.

6) Now take the last third of the pastry dough and roll that out large enough to cover the lid with extra to spare around the edges. Place to the side until required.

7) Place the drained potatoes in the base of the pie tin and spread them out equally. Do check there is no water with the potatoes as this will give you a soggy pastry base. There should be enough potato to nearly fill the tin. Sprinkle some extra seasoning in if you wish or even some dried herbs.

8) Now open a can of baked beans. To this add the soya sauce (tomatoes if using, finely diced) and stir. Pour over the potatoes and level out.

9) Dampen the edge of the pastry with water and place the pastry lid on top. With thumbs and forefingers work your way around the edge, pinching the edges against the edge of the tin to seal pastry layers together. You can then use an implement or end of a spoon handle to indent the edge to decorate.

10) Now using a sharp knife or scissors cut away the pastry excess around the edge and make three-five slits in the top so that air can escape.

11) Place in the middle of the oven that has been pre-heated and cook until golden round the edges.

Great served with a rich gravy.

STICKY FRUIT 'N' NUT CURRIED RICE

Time: 20 minutes cooking using pre-cooked rice

1 cup Brown Basmati Rice

1 cup Toasted Cashews

1 tablespoon Raw Coconut Oil

2 tablespoons Non-Dairy Margarine

2 Onions finely diced

2 Cloves Garlic finely diced

3–4 halves Sun-dried Tomatoes diced

¼ teaspoon Salt

1 Courgette diced

1 Bell Pepper diced

½ Large Bramley (Cooking) Apple finely diced

Handful Mixed Dried Fruit

1 teaspoon Soft Brown Sugar

1½ teaspoons Mild / Medium Curry Powder

1 tablespoon Lemon juice and Lemon for serving

Possibly water to loosen if becomes too thick.

1) Pre-cook the rice as instructed on the packet. Then drain and rinse with cold water to separate the grains. Leave to drain.

2) Toast the cashews by placing on a tin plate under a hot grill. Keep a careful watch they do not burn. You will smell them as they reach toasting point. You do not need to turn them over. Leave to the side.

3) Prepare the vegetables and apple by dicing small so that the final dish is delicate and pretty. You also want to achieve a multiple of flavours in each mouthful.

4) Dice the onion, garlic and tomatoes very small.

5) Melt the oil and margarine in a large frying pan. Add the onions, garlic, curry powder, lemon juice and salt and allow to sizzle until the onions start to brown slightly. Make sure the garlic doesn't burn, so keep heat low to medium.

6) Add the vegetables and apple and the dried fruit and stir thoroughly. You may want to add a tablespoon or two of water at this stage, rather like a stir fry, and place a lid on the pan and allow the vegetables to steam for a few minutes. You can also fry them instead. I do a little of both.

7) Finally I sprinkle the sugar, add the nuts and the rice and stir thoroughly. Allow the rice to heat through so it is all piping hot before you serve. If you want the rice really sticky add a little more water, place on the lid and allow to gently simmer for a few minutes. The rice will release starch and thicken the sauce.

STICKY FRUIT 'N' NUT CURRIED RICE

Tip: This is a hit with kids. It can be eaten as it is or as a side addition. But it really is so good on its own with some salad or bread. My son adores this in a wrap, and even has it cold the next day with a wrap and mayo.

MEDITERRANEAN STEW & HERB DUMPLINGS

Rich with four kinds of tomato and light, slightly salted, herb dumplings, this is a pleasure for the eyes as well as the taste-buds.

Time: 15 minutes prep and 30 minutes cooking. Feeds 4–6

- 4–6 tablespoons Olive Oil
- 2 large Onions, sliced
- 4–6 cloves Garlic, diced roughly
- Teaspoon Coarse Salt
- 3–4 Bell Peppers assorted colours, chopped roughly
- 2 Courgettes, chopped roughly
- 1 tablespoon mixed dried Herbs
- ½ tablespoon dried Rosemary
- 3–4 ripe plum Tomatoes, diced
- 4–6 halves Sun-dried Tomatoes in Oil, chopped finely
- 3 tablespoons Tomato Purée
- 350ml pack / tin of chopped tomatoes
- 120ml White Wine
- 250ml water
- Cornflour if required to thicken sauce (remember to add a little to its own cold water first before adding to the hot stew)
- Optional – Pecan Nuts and Chestnut Mushrooms
- Dumplings: see the Skills Section, doubling the amounts to make 10–12 dumplings. Add a teaspoon of mixed dried herbs to the dry ingredients before adding the water.

1) Make your dumplings first. These can then go into the fridge to chill. This always improves their final texture.

2) As always, prepare the vegetables. Everything can be nice and chunky, for a rustic and interesting stew. The only two ingredients I chop finely are the garlic and the sun-dried tomatoes.

3) Warm the olive oil in a large pan (a stock pot is best) and add the garlic and onion, salt and stir. Sizzle for the onions to soften a little.

4) Add the peppers and the fresh tomatoes you have chopped. Stir and allow to cook for about 5 minutes.

5) Add the courgettes and the herbs. Stir and allow to cook for a further 2–3 minutes.

6) Now add everything else. Stir thoroughly and bring to the boil.

7) Once boiling turn the heat down so it is simmering well, stir again and then place the dumplings onto the surface of the stew. Don't worry if they sink to their middles, but don't let them sink completely – you will need to thicken the sauce or remove some if they do that. **Put the lid on and DON'T REMOVE IT for 20–25 minutes while the**

dumplings steam. If you think the stew is boiling too fiercely, just turn it down a little, but don't lift the lid.

8) After 20–25 minutes the dumplings can be lifted out and placed on a warm plate while you stir up the stew and check its thickness. If it needs cornflour you can add this now (added to a little of its own cold water). Allow it to cook for a minute or two before serving.

THREE BEAN CURRY

This is taken from a slow-cooker recipe called Goan Curry. It is pretty well changed beyond recognition here, but the idea of mixing various beans and lentils still interests me. This form of cooking retains the individuality of the pulses whereas slow cooking tends to blend them all into a homogenised mass.

Time: Prep around 30 minutes; cooking around 30 minutes.* Makes a large pot feeding 4–6 adults

3 tablespoons Raw Coconut Oil

2 large Onions (red or white), sliced and diced

2" piece of fresh Ginger, diced finely

6 cloves Garlic, diced finely

1 small Chilli (optional), diced finely, seeds removed

...

1½ teaspoon Ground Cumin

2 teaspoons Ground Coriander

1 tablespoon Turmeric

Optional Curry Powder if you wish but not authentic for this dish.

...

2 tablespoons Raw Cane Sugar / Dark Brown Sugar – Soft Brown will do

1 teaspoon coarse Sea Salt

2 tablespoons Lemon juice

3 Plum Tomatoes diced

2 tablespoons Tomato Purée / paste

...

6 cups / 1.4 litres water

½ cup Red Lentils washed and drained

200g Stringless Runner Beans / Green Beans sliced and diced

...

Up to 1 tablespoon Cornflour in a little water (this is not in the authentic version, but I like my sauce thicker or it is a little watery)

...

6–8 cups of Pre-Cooked Beans of various sorts.

1 cup / 240ml Soya Plain Yoghurt or Cream

1) First I suggest you prepare all of the ingredients into their separate groupings as shown in the ingredients listing. The vegetables, and ginger, need to be diced very small. Place each grouping into a separate bowl.

2) Melt the oil in a large lidded stock pot and add the onion, garlic and ginger and gently sizzle these until soft.

3) Add the chilli if you are using and the spices. Allow them to sizzle and their flavours to bloom. This takes a couple of minutes – don't worry if they seem to stick to the pan as you stir them.

4) Add the sugar, salt and lemon juice along with the plum tomatoes and the Purée. Stir thoroughly.

5) Now add the water, red lentils and the green beans. Stir then place the lid on the pot.

6) Bring to the boil and simmer rapidly for ten minutes. Then turn down the heat and simmer gently until the lentils are very soft.

7) Add the cornflour (in water) to the pot and stir thoroughly as you do so. It will thicken the sauce slightly.

8) Add the beans you have chosen and stir. Add the yoghurt or cream, stir and allow the whole dish to come back to the boil. Simmer for a couple of minutes to make sure the cornflour is properly cooked.

* At first, the preparation will take around 30 minutes, but you will get quicker with practice. Although the cooking time can be very quick at around 30 minutes, cooking for longer will give better flavour.

SWEET CHILLI VEGETABLES
& Wholewheat Noodles

Time: 20–30 minutes. Feeds 3–4

1 tablespoon Coconut oil
1 tablespoon Non-Dairy Margarine
2–3 small strong Onions or 5–6 Large Spring Onions, diced
3 cloves Garlic, finely diced
Small piece of fresh Ginger, finely diced
¼ teaspoon Sea Salt & Pepper
½ teaspoon Paprika
1 teaspoon Mild Chilli Powder
1 tablespoon Tomato Purée
1 tablespoon Soft Brown Sugar
½ tablespoon Dark Soya Sauce
Juice ½ Lime or Lemon
2 tablespoons White Wine
125ml / ½ cup water
1-2 Bell Peppers, finely sliced
1–2 medium Courgettes, finely sliced
1 Carrot, finely sliced
¼ cup / handful frozen Sweetcorn
½ teaspoon Cornflour (optional)
Wholewheat Noodles

1) Chop all of the vegetables small and keep to the side. Check how long your noodles take by checking packaging. Make sure you have boiling water ready to hand. I usually start cooking the vegetables once the noodles are in their water.

2) Melt the oil and margarine in a saucepan or frying pan. Add the garlic, ginger and onions and sizzle until soft and beginning to brown.

3) Add seasonings and spices allowing them to sizzle for a couple of minutes.

4) Now add the sugar, tomato purée, soya sauce, lemon/lime juice, white wine and water and bring to a rapid simmer.

5) Add the vegetables and simmer for no more than 2 minutes so they stay crisp and firm. Add cornflour mixed with a little water to thick the sauce if you wish.

COTTAGE PIE

Time: Prep 15 minutes, total cooking time 30 minutes

8–10 medium white Potatoes, enough that when mashed will cover the surface of the cooking dish. Peeled and chopped small.

Non-Dairy Margarine for mashing potatoes

2 tablespoons Nutritional Yeast flakes (to be added to the potatoes when mashing; optional – you won't be able to taste it)

1 x 415g tin of Baked Beans

½ Cauliflower cut into very small florets

½ Broccoli Head cut into very small florets

1 cup finely chopped Swede (optional)

1 large Onion sliced

2 cloves Garlic finely diced

3 tablespoons Non-Dairy Margarine

2 tablespoons Tomato Purée

1 cup / 240ml boiling water

½ teaspoon dried Herbs

Salt and Pepper

Enriching Gravy composed of;
   6 Sweet Chestnuts (ready cooked)
   1 tablespoon Dark Soya Sauce
   ½ teaspoon Marmite
   ½ cup / 120ml boiling water
   ½ teaspoon Cornflour
   ½ tablespoon Lemon juice

1) Peel and slice potatoes, rinse and place in saucepan of fresh water with a little salt. Bring to the boil then set to simmer.

2) Prepare the florets of cauliflower and broccoli, breaking them up into very small pieces and peel and chop the swede finely. Put to one side.

3) Peel and dice the garlic and onion and place in a large saucepan where the margarine has been melted. Gently fry in the margarine until the onion begins to brown.

4) Add the vegetables, tomato purée and the boiling water and stir well. Bring to the boil, then turn to gentle simmer, place lid on and leave for 15 minutes.

5) Whilst the vegetables are cooking, prepare the enriching gravy by placing all of the ingredients into a blender and blending until smooth.

6) After 15 minutes check the potatoes and turn off heat if they are tender. Drain and leave to one side.

7) Now add the enriching gravy (previously blitzing all the ingredients for this in a small processor) and stir thoroughly. Also add the baked beans. I always drain off the bean juice on the top but you can add this if you choose.

COTTAGE PIE

8) Bring back to boil, then turn down low, replace the lid and let it all gently simmer. If the mixture is still pretty runny then leave the lid off so some of the moisture evaporates away and it thickens the mix. You can always add more cornflour or some nutritional yeast which will enrich and thicken the gravy.

9) Mash the potatoes with a little margarine, adding the nutritional yeast, and a little freshly ground pepper. The yeast dries the potatoes so they become crisp quicker.

10) Check the vegetables are cooked through, but not mushy. Now pour all of the vegetable, bean and gravy mixture into the oven-proof dish and level. Leave to cool for 5 minutes so a slight skin forms.

11) Add the mashed potatoes gently to the surface of the gravy mixture, a teaspoon at a time. I do this by scooping up a dessert spoonful and scraping teaspoon amounts off with another spoon. This stops large lumps of potato sinking through the gravy. Don't press the potato down at all, just let it sit on the surface as much as possible.

12) Finally, place the whole thing under a hot grill and crisp up the top. This is my favourite bit of the dish!

This can be made and chilled to be cooked later. You will need an oven proof dish approx. 24 x 26 x 10 cm.

Tip: If you are freezing or chilling... You can leave adding the potato until later if you are chilling it. Freezing it is better to only freeze the bean and veg mixture cooked, and make the mashed potatoes fresh on the day you are having the meal. Re-heat the bean and veg mixture then place in an oven proof dish and top with potatoes.

RICH NUT LOAF

Time: 20 minutes prep, cooking 55 minutes in one tin, 35 minutes two tins. Oven 180°C. Serves 6

¾ cup Pecans
¾ cup Plain Cashews
½ cup Roasted Hazelnuts
3 slices Brown / Wholemeal / Seeded Bread, crumbed
1 teaspoon mixed dried herbs
4 sprigs fresh Flat Leaf Parsley chopped finely (without stalks)
2–4 Sun-dried Tomato halves, chopped finely
¼ cup Soya Flour

Salt and pepper
1 small strong Onion, finely diced
2 small cloves Garlic, finely diced
2 Tomatoes, chopped
1 tablespoon Oil
¼ cup Wholemeal Flour
¼ pint / ⅔ cup cold water
½ Lemon, juiced
¼ teaspoon Marmite / Vegemite
½ tablespoon Dark Soya Sauce

1) In a large mixing bowl place the breadcrumbs, herbs, salt, pepper and soya flour.

2) In a processor, blitz the nuts until broken into very small pieces but not completely to dust, or there will be no texture to your loaf. You may prefer to put them into a tea towel and bash with a rolling pin.

3) Add the crushed nuts to the mixing bowl.

4) Dice the onion, garlic, tomatoes and dried tomatoes and leave to the side.

5) In a frying pan place the oil and warm. Add the onion and garlic and sauté until soft. Add the tomatoes (fresh and dried) and stir, cooking gently to soften and release the juices.

6) Once the tomatoes become mushy, add the lemon juice, dark soya sauce and Marmite, stirring well.

7) Then sprinkle the wholemeal flour over the whole contents of the frying pan. Add the water gradually, stirring as you do so to avoid clumping. Add all the water so that you end up with a thick paste in the pan.

8) Now add this paste to the dry ingredients in the mixing bowl. Stir it all together very thoroughly.

9) Spoon all the mixture into a greased (with margarine) 1 lb or 500g bread tin, or into two small bread tins. Pat the mixture down flat, and pressing it so it forms a dense loaf. I always make two small loaves so I can freeze one.

10) Pop into oven on middle shelf and cook until a knife comes out of the centre cleanly.

RICH NUT LOAF

11) Allow to cool for 10 minutes in the tin before turning out.

Tip: For best results, cook the previous day and chill in the fridge. Cut into slices while cold, and then wrap in baking foil and re-heat. This gives nice neat slices and avoids crumbling or braking up of the nut pieces.

Tip: Good with salad or gravy, hot or cold. One of my friends has it for breakfast! Full of protein, nut oils and good carbs. Low in bad fats and sugar.

Tip: Makes a great filling for peppers, mixed with rice. Use ready cooked nut loaf broken up, add cooked rice and place in ready-soaked peppers, as per 'Mini Stuffed Peppers' dish.

Tip: This is great frozen once cooked. It is then available for quick easy meals any way you like.

COCONUT & LIME CURRY
with Cauliflower & Sweet Potatoes

Time: 30 minutes prep, cooking 20 minutes. Serves 4–6

50g / 2 oz Non-Dairy butter
1 large Onion finely diced
2 large cloves garlic finely diced
1½ cm fresh Ginger, peeled and finely diced

...

3 green Cardamom Pods, slightly crushed
1 Bay leaf
½ teaspoon ground Fenugreek
1 teaspoon ground Coriander
1 teaspoon Balti Mix
½ teaspoon Turmeric
½ teaspoon Salt
Pinch dried crushed Chillies (or more if you like heat. You can replace this with chilli powder, but take care as it is very hot)

1 tablespoon Tomato Paste / Purée
½ Lime, juiced

...

3 tablespoons Desiccated unsweetened Coconut
3 tablespoons ground Almonds
2 teaspoons Soft Brown Sugar

...

1 Cauliflower broken into whole florets
1 large Sweet Potato peeled and chopped into small cubes

...

½ cup Frozen Sweetcorn
Handful of frozen Green Peas
1 cup Coconut Cream (or ordinary)
2 cup water
1 teaspoon Cornflour

1) Indian cooking is about preparation and order of ingredients. The first thing to do is take each group of ingredients (placed between the dotted lines), dice and measure out and place into a separate bowl, ready for cooking. Break the cauliflower up and place in a pan with water. Bring to the boil and then strain. Leave to the side.

2) Add to the cauliflower the sweet potato, peeled and diced into small cubes. That does not need boiling as it cooks quickly.

3) Have sweetcorn, peas, coconut cream and cornflour to hand.

4) Place the butter in a large pan (biggest you have) and gently warm it. Don't let it burn.

5) Add first the onion, garlic and ginger, stir and turn the heat up a little to soften them. Let them cook until the onions start to brown.

COCONUT & LIME CURRY

6) Now add all your spices, pods and leaves. Turn the heat up a little and stir constantly. It should sizzle and the flavours and oils will be released from the spices at this stage. This is called 'blooming'. It is the stage that makes the flavour work! Takes no more than 4–5 minutes, tops.

7) Turn the heat down a little now and add the lime juice, and the tomato Purée. Stir well as it will stick a little. Don't worry it will lift when you add water in a minute.

8) Add the coconut, almonds and sugar, stirring well and allowing the coconut and almonds to absorb the oil and flavours, then add the water and stir.

9) Add the cauliflower and sweet potato, place a lid on the pan and bring to the boil. Then simmer for 5 minutes.

10) Add all that you have left, including cornflour which will need to be mixed with a tablespoon of water first. If your coconut cream is very solid in its carton, don't worry – it goes to liquid on heating.

11) You add your frozen veg. Replace lid and on a very low heat simmer another five minutes.

12) Check the cauliflower to make sure it is tender but not over soft. It is best when it retains a little firmness. The curry is ready to serve.

Tip: If you are cooking this intending to freeze it all, then do not cook for the last five minutes of stage 11. Freezing and thawing will soften the vegetable tissues and re-heating will do the cooking you need.

Tip: Try this dish with some toasted cashews added, or nuts and seeds of your choice. Is also lovely with large chunks of courgette.

This dish will supply you with the spices that are the most versatile in my kitchen. You will find uses for them from now on.

RED RICE & POLENTA BURGERS

RED RICE & POLENTA BURGERS

These might sound a bit overly-vegan, but believe me they are the best! My son believes them to be as satisfying as the old meat alternative he used to enjoy, and with chilli sauce are a knock-out!

Time: pre-cooking rice and polenta 25 minutes, the burgers 20 minutes. Makes 6–8 burgers

100g Red Rice / Brown Rice cooked, drained and cooled

50g Polenta, cooked and cooled

Generous bunch of Chives, finely diced (I use scissors)

3–5 leaves of Spring Greens or Green Cabbage, stalks removed and finely sliced

2 halves Sun-dried Tomato in oil, diced

Generous Salt & Pepper

Zest of one whole Lemon

1 cm fresh Ginger, finely diced

1 large slice Wholemeal Granary bread, crumbed finely

Pinch Garlic Salt

½ teaspoon dried Marjoram

Oil for frying

1) Pre-cook the rice and the polenta and leave both to cool.

2) Chop finely the chives, the greens (remove stalks then roll the leaves up together like a newspaper and cut across finely), the dried tomatoes and the ginger.

3) Crumb the slice of bread in a processor.

4) Now place all the above ingredients into a mixing bowl and add to this the seasonings and zest. Mix everything together using your hands until all is thoroughly blended.

5) Taking a ball of the mixture roughly the size of a clementine, squeeze the mixture together in your hands and then flatten between your palms, working around the edges to keep the burger nice and neat. The burgers need to be about 8–10 mm thick. Place all the burgers on a plate – at this stage you can cover and refrigerate them.

6) When ready to cook place 1–2 tablespoons oil in a frying pan, heat until hot and place all the burgers in. Make sure they sizzle. Fry until both sides of the burgers are golden and crisp.

These can be made and chilled in advance.

CLASSIC CHILLI BEAN BURGER

These are my own take on a classic, with addition of oats and oily dried tomatoes which give a great depth to the flavour.

Time: 30–60 minutes. Oven 190°C. Makes 6

- 380g pack ready cooked Black Beans (230g bean weight)
- 1 cup frozen Sweetcorn, defrosted
- 1 cup Rolled Oats
- 2 tablespoons Tomato Purée
- 1 slice of bread, crumbed
- 1 small Onion, finely diced
- Juice of ½ Lemon
- 4 Sun-dried Tomato halves (in oil), finely chopped
- 2–3 Medjool dates, finely chopped
- ½ teaspoon Garlic Salt
- 1 teaspoon dried mixed Herbs
- 2 teaspoons Mild Chilli Powder
- ½ teaspoon Cajun spice
- ¼ teaspoon crushed dried Chillies
- Salt
- Oil for frying

1) Drain and rinse the beans. Place half of them in a large mixing bowl and keep the other half to the side.

2) Chop the dates and sun-dried tomatoes very small and add to the beans. Crumb the bread in a processor and add to the mixing bowl along with everything else – apart from the beans you placed to the side.

3) Use your hands to mulch and massage all of the ingredients together, squashing the beans so they help to bring everything together in a semi-dry semi-sticky mass.

4) Now mix in the rest of the beans gently to retain their shape. Roughly separate the mix into six balls and begin to make the burgers by taking each ball and compressing it. Then flatten it between your hands and fashion the edges so it makes a neat dense burger. The denser it is the better.

5) Once you have done this with all of the mixture, place the burgers in the fridge for 30 minutes if you have the time.

6) When ready to eat, first fry the burgers in hot oil for two minutes each side (or longer if you want them crunchier) then place them on a baking sheet and bake in the hot oven (190°C) for 10–15 minutes to assure they are hot and cooked through.

Great served with Raita, Grilled Courgettes, Coleslaw, Smoked Paprika Chips or salad – all available in this book!

Tip: You could make a batch of 12 by doubling up the ingredients and freezing half of them uncooked for a later date.

If you do this, keep the burgers separated by placing a small piece of baking parchment between them and defrost before frying.

CAJUN & GINGER BURGERS

Time: 30 minutes prep, 8–10 minutes frying time. Makes 8 small patties

- ¼ cup raw Quinoa, rinsed, cooked and drained
- 1 large Carrot, finely grated and patted between kitchen paper to remove some water
- 1–2 slices fresh Wholemeal / Seeded Bread, crumbed in processor
- 2 tablespoons Ground Golden Flax Seeds (optional)
- 2 tablespoons Tomato Purée
- 1 small Onion and 1 small clove Garlic and ½cm fresh Ginger, all diced finely
- Juice of one Lime and a little zest (or Lemon)
- 1 tablespoon light Soya Sauce
- ½ teaspoon Cajun Spice plus pinch of good Salt
- Sprig of fresh Flat Leaf Parsley or other herb like Sage or Basil
- Tablespoon Non-Dairy Margarine
- Oil for frying

1) In a large mixing bowl place quinoa, carrot, flax, parsley (or other), breadcrumbs, Cajun spice and salt.

2) In frying pan pop in the margarine and melt. Then add the diced onion, garlic and ginger and sauté until soft.

3) Add the lemon juice, zest, tomato Purée, soya sauce and stir together, for one minute.

4) Add the pan mixture to the dry ingredients in the mixing bowl. Mix together well. Best to use your hands.

5) Taking a portion of the mixture about the size of a small kiwi, press together and shape into a small burger, making sure you press the edges round. If the mixture is impossibly sticky, add some more bread crumbs.

6) Fry burgers in shallow hot oil. If oil not hot enough the patties will just soak it all up and become soggy. Cook until very golden then gently flip over. Cook until both sides are crisp. Sit them on some kitchen towel before serving.

GARAM MASALA LENTIL STEW

Great use of left-overs in the fridge.

Time: 1 hour soaking time, 30 minus prep, 30 mins cooking. Feeds 4 with a side dish

1 cup Lentils soaked for an hour (I use Yellow Split lentils or 'Chana Dal')

Enough water to cook the lentils in (see packaging for advice).

...

2 tablespoons Raw Coconut Oil

2 tablespoons Non-Dairy Margarine

2 white Onions, diced

3–4 cloves Garlic, finely diced

...

½ tablespoon medium heat Curry Powder

1 teaspoon Turmeric

1 Bay Leaf

1 Star Anise (or ½ teaspoon Fennel seeds)

1 teaspoon Paprika

2 teaspoons Garam Masala

1 teaspoon Coarse Salt

...

5 Ripe Plum Tomatoes, chopped

1–2 large Portobello Mushrooms, roughly chopped

...

2 leaves fresh Sage, chopped finely

2 tablespoons Tomato Purée

2 tablespoons Lemon Juice

2 tablespoons Soft Brown Sugar

3 tablespoons Red Wine

1 tablespoon Sherry Vinegar

...

¼ Cauliflower cut into florets

½ Bell Pepper, roughly chopped

½ Courgette, roughly chopped

Any other fridge left-overs such as cooked potatoes.

Large handful Mixed Dried Fruit

...

60–80ml Non-Dairy Cream or Yoghurt

What matters here is preparing all of the ingredients.

Thoroughly rinse your lentils until water runs clear. Then soak them in boiling water for a minimum of an hour. If using whole or long cook lentils, partially cook them before using them. This speeds up the cooking of the curry. See the lentil packaging for advice on cooking times.

1) Sort each group of ingredients into separate bowls ready for cooking. Dice the first group of vegetables small. The last group of vegetables can be chunkier.

2) Partly pre-cook the lentils. Keep them handy still in their cooking water.

3) Melt the margarine and coconut oil in a large lidded pan. Add the onions and garlic and sizzle for a couple of minutes.

MAIN DISHES

4) Add the seasonings, spices and seeds and the bay leaf. Allow the spices and seeds to sizzle until the seeds start to 'pop'.

5) Add the plum tomatoes and mushrooms, all diced reasonably chunky, and stir well. Now add the fresh sage, purée, lemon juice, sugar, wine and vinegar and stir to lift the spices off the bottom of the pot.

6) Now add the lentils with their water and bring to the boil. Rapidly boil for ten minutes, then reduce heat to a constant simmer. Place the lid on and simmer until lentils are virtually tender.

7) Take the vegetables, dried fruit and any left-overs in the fridge and add these to the pot. Bring back to the boil then reduce heat to simmer around 12–15 minutes so that the cauliflower is tender, but not mushy. By now the lentils should be cooked – it is the lentils that you need to check and the cooking of everything else is timed against this.

8) With a hand blender partially blend to form a thicker sauce, then add the cream or yoghurt. Now it is ready to serve.

Tip: This is a good dish to use up any left over ratatouille.

MUSHROOM & BROCCOLI PIE

Broccoli can be replaced by cauliflower and/or other vegetables. Great with gravy or with ketchup.

Time: 1 hour 30 minutes prep and cooking. Oven 190°C

To make 4 x 4½" pies in loose bottomed tins or one 8" pie in a spring-form tin.

Pastry:
- 250g / 10 oz Plain Flour
- 75g / 3 oz Vegetable Suet
- 50g / 2 oz Non-Dairy Margarine
- Generous pinch Salt (up to ¼ teaspoon)
- 5–6 tablespoons cold Water

Filling:
- 220g / 9 oz Button Mushrooms cut into quarters
- 300g Broccoli Florets, cut small
- 2 Tomatoes finely chopped
- 300ml / ½ pint Vegetable Stock
- 1 Onion finely sliced
- 1½ tablespoons Vegetable Oil
- 10 leaves of fresh Rosemary
- 6 Chives
- 2 tablespoons Light Soya Sauce
- 2 tablespoons Red or White Cooking Wine
- ½ teaspoon Mixed Dried Herbs
- 1 teaspoon Paprika
- 1 teaspoon Marmite
- 2 teaspoons Cornflour
- Generous grind of Black Pepper
- Optional addition of ¼ partly cooked Swede, or some sliced Sweet Chestnuts

1) Make the pastry and line the tins first. Place the flour and fats into a mixing bowl with generous salt and mix together with your finger-tips. Add the water and mix this through with your fingertips. Then begin to squeeze the mixture together and see if it will form a ball. If not break it up and add a tiny amount of water and try again. Once you can make a cohesive ball it is ready. Unlike shortcrust pastry, re-forming suet dough will not make it tough.

2) Divide the ball into four equal amounts if you are making the small pies. You need to make both a bottom and top for each of your pie tins. The best way to do this is to take each portion and split it again into two-thirds and a third. The two-thirds portion is then rolled out as the base and sides of the tin. The last third will be rolled out as the lid of the pie. If you are making one large pie, split the dough into three, using two thirds for the base and the last third for the lid.

MUSHROOM & BROCCOLI PIE

3) Once your tins are lined and have a top to go with them, pop them into the fridge to chill while you make the filling.

4) Place the margarine into a frying pan and melt. Gently fry the mushrooms cut into smaller pieces and the onion, diced, until they are softened and the mushrooms are giving out water. When a mushroom releases water it means it is cooked.

5) Place the whole contents of the frying pan into a large saucepan, along with all the other ingredients EXCEPT for the cornflour. Make sure the broccoli florets are quite small – the same size as the mushroom pieces.

6) Bring everything to the boil, then turn down to a gentle heat, place the lid on top and allow to simmer until the broccoli is tender.

7) In a cup place the cornflour with a touch of cold water and mix to make a milky liquid. Add this to the vegetables stirring it continually as the gravy thickens. If you want a thicker mixture just add a little more cornflour the same way.

8) Now you can fill your pastry with the filling.

9) Dampen the edges of the pastry and press on the pastry lid. Squeeze the edges together and if you like roll them over a little to form a rolled crust. Trim off any excess before you do this or there will be too much pastry!

10) Make a couple of slits with the tip of the knife in the top of each pie and place on a baking sheet. On the middle shelf bake until golden around the edges.

Tip: It's good to make a gravy to go with this dish.

STEW & DUMPLINGS

For stew lovers, I cannot stress enough how GOOD this is! It took some doing to get it right, but this is the Queen of vegan stew and dumplings in the British style. Please give it a try and don't be afraid of doing dumplings.

Time: total 1 hour and 15 minutes. Feeds 4

- 2 tablespoons Non-Dairy Margarine
- 2 Onions, sliced thinly
- 1 clove Garlic, diced finely
- ½ Cooking Apple, skinned and diced
- 300g Mushrooms (preferably Mini Portobello or Chestnut cut into large pieces)
- 1 Courgette, diced
- Handful Pearl Barley
- 250ml Vegetable Stock plus 100ml water for later
- 2 handfuls of Cashews toasted under the grill
- 6–8 small New Potatoes, chopped small (or small White all year round ones)
- 2 ripe Plum Tomatoes, chopped (or small can)
- 2 tablespoons Tomato Purée
- 3 halves Sun-dried Tomatoes, diced
- 3 leaves fresh Sage (or ½ teaspoon dried)
- ½ tablespoon dried Marjoram
- 1 teaspoon Paprika
- Salt & Pepper
- 1 tablespoon Dark Soya Sauce
- 4 tablespoons Red Cooking Wine
- ½ tablespoon Cornflour to thicken (this will depend how much water is released by the mushrooms and how thick you like your stew)
- For Dumplings see the instructions in the Skill Set section (page 28). Make these before you need them and place in the fridge. They go fluffier this way.

(Prepare your dumplings and chill.)

1) Prepare the vegetables and mushrooms first to the size you like. Prepare the potatoes by cutting them small (small bite-size pieces) and then rinsing them. They need to be par-boiled (brought to the boil) then drained and left ready. Try to keep the skins on if they are young potatoes.

2) Toast the cashews by placing on a baking tray under a medium hot grill. They brown quickly so keep watch!

3) Prepare the onion as thin strips and the garlic finely diced. The apple must be peeled and cut into small chunks.

4) Melt the margarine and add the salt, the onions, garlic and apple. Allow to gently sizzle until soft and beginning to colour.

STEW & DUMPLINGS

5) Add the courgettes, tomatoes and the seasonings and herbs, stirring well. Allow to cook for a couple of minutes so the courgettes take up some of the margarine and flavours.

6) Add the mushrooms, the tomato purée and the red wine. Stir thoroughly and turn the heat down and allow the mushrooms to begin to sweat. Do this with the lid on for about 4 minutes. Make sure the heat is not too high.

7) Now add the veg stock, pearl barley, potatoes and all other ingredients apart from the cashews and the cornflour. At this point you may need to add the extra water to make sure that the potatoes have enough to cook in.

8) Stir, place the lid on and bring to the boil. Then gently simmer for 10 minutes.

9) After 10 minutes, add the cashews and the cornflour, which will need to be added to a little water of its own to form a runny paste before being added – make sure you stir thoroughly as you gradually add the cornflour. You may need more or less, depending on how thick you want the resultant stew.

10) I usually prepare the stew earlier in the day and turn off the heat at this point, leaving the pot to stand. I then heat it through thoroughly later on. This means the flavours are richer and the dumplings – which I also prepare at the same time, have been in the fridge long enough to be chilled through.

11) When ready to eat, reheat the stew to boiling, then turn heat down to rapid simmer and place all of the dumplings on its surface – replace the lid and leave for 30 minutes. **One word here is that if you like your stew thick, thicken AFTER you have cooked the dumplings or the bottom of your stew may burn while the dumplings are cooking. NEVER lift the lid when dumplings are cooking.**

Tip: Another good addition if you don't like dumplings is to make a piece of short crust pastry with generous salt in it, on an oven proof plate or dish and serve a slice with the stew. Just pop into the oven at 190°C for 10–12 minutes.

Wholewheat Noodles are good too, and Wheatberries.

LASAGNE

A very tasty light version of the original. This makes a small one for two to three adults; simply double up the ingredients to make a family-size one.

Time: 30 minutes prep then 10 minutes assemblage and 40 minutes baking time. Oven 170–180°C

Filling:

2 tablespoons Non-Dairy Margarine

Generous pinch Salt

2 Onions, thinly sliced

2 cloves Garlic, finely diced

2 medium Courgettes, diced small

3 large ripe Plum Tomatoes, diced small

350g Mushrooms (Mini Portobello or Chestnut), chopped small

2 tablespoons Tomato Purée

1–2 tablespoon Red Wine

½ tablespoon dried Marjoram

½ tablespoon dried Basil

1 teaspoon dried Tarragon

White Sauce:

150ml Non-Dairy Cream

200ml Non-Dairy milk (use a Nut milk for extra richness)

Generous Salt & Pepper

1 tablespoon Non-Dairy Margarine

1 tablespoon Cornflour

2–4 tablespoons Nutritional Yeast (or vegan hard cheese)

6–8 sheets of Lasagne Pasta (whole wheat is really good)

1) Prepare the vegetables. I like to cut everything small, but you can cut as you like.

2) Melt the margarine in a pan with a lid and fry the onions and garlic. Once softened add the courgettes and sizzle for 2–3 minutes.

3) Now add all the rest of the ingredients for the savoury filling, stirring and bring to the boil. Reduce heat to a simmer and with the lid on, simmer gently until everything is tender and the sauce has darkened. If the sauce seems a bit runny, simply remove the pan lid and simmer for a few minutes more. This will release some of the water and thicken the sauce up a little more.

4) To prepare the sauce, simply place all the ingredients into a saucepan and with a hand whisk (non-electric) stir whilst gently heating to boiling. This is a fail-safe way to make sauce without lumps. Once it is thickened you are ready to assemble the lasagne.

5) In a 1½ litre / 2 pint oven proof dish, place a third of the savoury mixture and spread evenly. Then place a single layer of lasagne pasta sheets over it. On top of the lasagne spoon a third of the sauce, spreading it evenly over the pasta sheets.

6) Now repeat step 5 two more times so you end up with three layers, ending with the sauce on top.

7) Place on the middle shelf of your pre-heated oven and bake for 30–40 minutes until a knife will go through all of the pasta layers easily.

To serve, use a sharp knife tip to cut through and assign portions that can be lifted out with a large spoon or a fish slice.

STIR-FRY VEGETABLES WITH TOASTED PEANUTS

Time: 10–15 minutes

Stir-fry sauce, pre-made (see Stir-Fry Sauces, page 104) or shop bought

A selection of vegetables that have colour and crunch.

Include an Onion for flavour.

Some unsalted Peanuts (or other nut)

A little oil

Some noodles or spaghetti

1) Prepare all of your vegetables first. Cut them into varying lengths and sizes and do try and use an array of colours as stir-fries are very attractive when this is considered. Include things like spring onions, radish, and sweet corn as well as the traditional beansprouts, carrot and pepper.

2) Make sure you know how to cook your noodles or spaghetti and when to put this on to boil. The stir-fry takes about 5 minutes so time it to coincide if you can. This avoids over-cooking the vegetables.

3) Place oil in a large frying pan with a lid preferably, and start by cooking the onion, peppers, carrot, celery, green beans – anything that is quite tough and crunchy. Toss on a high heat for a minute.

4) Now add anything a little more tender like spring onion or small sliced mushrooms and stir again.

5) Add 2 tablespoons of the noodle/spaghetti water to the vegetables and place the lid on so they steam a little. Pop the lid on or cover with foil and leave for 1–2 minutes. You will need to turn the heat down to half.

6) Now take off the lid, add the nuts and the sauce and stir. Turn the heat down a little more, replace the lid and sort out draining your noodles/spaghetti.

7) Serve stir fry and enjoy the amazing freshness of simple aromatic food.

MAIN DISHES

WINTER VEGETABLE PIE

So comforting on a Winter's evening. A rustic pie packed with rich flavours and gravy. Making it square also adds a little novelty.

Time: 20 minutes prep, 45 minutes baking time. Feeds 4

WINTER VEGETABLE PIE

Pastry:

250g / 10 oz Plain Flour

75g / 3 oz Vegetable Suet

50g / 2 oz Non-Dairy Margarine

Generous pinch salt

4–5 tablespoons cold water

Pie filling:

500g Mushrooms (Dark ones are best, so Portobello or Chestnut)

250g peeled and finely diced Swede

1 large Carrot, diced

2 ripe Plum Tomatoes, chopped

2 Onions, sliced

1 clove Garlic, finely chopped

3 tablespoons Non-Dairy Margarine

1 teaspoon Dried Mixed Herbs

250ml Vegetable Stock (or the cooking water for the root vegetables)

For the pie gravy; (the following needs to be blended together)

1 tablespoon Dark Soya Sauce	½ tablespoon Cornflour
2 halves Sun-dried Tomatoes in Oil	1 teaspoon paprika
1 tablespoon Red Wine Vinegar	120ml COLD Water
6–8 Ready Cooked Sweet Chestnuts	10 Blackberries (optional)
Salt & Pepper	

1) Prepare the pastry as shown in the Skills Section 'Making Vegan Suet Pastry' (page 30) and line your pie dish/tin with it. Keep the portion intended for the pie lid as a ball in the tin and put the tin in the fridge to chill while you make the filling.

2) Peel the swede and cut into small narrow strips, and then dice. Cover with water in a small saucepan and bring to the boil. Drain (keep the water to use as stock) and keep to the side. If you use turnips and/or parsnips do the same with these.

3) Melt the margarine in a large lidded saucepan and fry the onions and garlic until soft. Add the tomatoes and the mushrooms and stir. Allow to simmer gently with lid on for 3–4 minutes.

4) Now add the stock with the pre-boiled vegetables (the water you boiled them in can be used as the stock), herbs and seasoning. Place the lid on and allow to simmer gently until the root vegetables are tender but not mushy.

5) While the vegetables are cooking, make the pie gravy. Place all the ingredients listed into a small blender/processor or a jug using a hand blender. This includes the cornflour. Make sure the water you use is cold or the cornflour will create lumps. Blend until smooth. If using a hand blender, don't worry if you are left with bits floating in the liquid. That is fine.

6) Add the gravy to the pot and stir thoroughly as you bring back to the boil. The whole thing will become rich and thicken slightly. For thicker result add more cornflour in a little of its own cold water.

7) Make sure your oven is pre-heating as you make the pie. Take the pie tin and remove the ball of pastry, rolling it out ready as the pie lid. Pour the savoury filling into the pie, wet the edges of the pastry with water and place the pastry lid on top. Press the pastry edges to seal and then use the end of a spoon handle to press and mark around the edge. Trim off excess pastry from the edges and pierce the pie three of four times with a sharp knife.

8) Bake on the middle shelf for 45 minutes. Serve hot.

Use a 26cm diagonal tray bake tin, or a 3 litre/2½ pint oven proof pie dish. This pie is best when made quite deep.

Tip: I like to drain off some of the pie gravy from the pot just before filling the pie, and use this as extra gravy drizzled over the pie on the plate or over vegetables served alongside.

Tip: Another way to finish the pie edge is to press together the lid and lip of base and then fold or roll the edge to give a double crust. It is a rustic look, as can be seen in the photo.

SWEET DELIGHTS

Cakes, cookies, tarts, whips and puddings!

MOIST CHOCOLATE SPONGE TRAY BAKE

STRAWBERRY FRUIT SMOOTHIE

FRUIT SMOOTHIES

These should not be forgotten as they make amazing breakfasts and desserts as well as a nutritious drink all of their own. I was not a fan of fruit smoothies myself, as most seemed to have banana in them and I can be a bit fussy about the taste and texture of banana.

Once I got my blender that all changed. I became so busy with writing this book, I found I wasn't eating as well as I had, and needed a way to prepare and ingest lots of goodness in a matter of minutes. Well the raw and beautiful goodness in these tasty drinks is the answer (actually I am going to go do one right now).

You can put anything in them, quite literally. As long as you remember the rule about blending – put the liquid in first, then the soft fruits and leave the seeds and icecubes last – and always blend on 'low' or 'pulse' setting first.

My favourite at the moment is simply pineapple and blueberries, with a quarter of a glass of soya milk and a handful of Golden Flax seed. The one shown here also has strawberries in it. I have also started adding a handful of raw baby leaf spinach, a must for iron and vitamin B. Also use fruit juice in place of milk. Try using your own homemade milks too.

The Fat Boy Smoothie

Great for a breakfast, as a weight-gain drink or after a training session, this is packed with good calories – that means full of nutrition as well as energy. Take care; this drink packs in 750–850 calories and contains approx. 57% of a man's RDA of fat, 77% of which is saturated. To reduce this, replace the coconut cream with coconut milk.

400ml Oat Milk
50ml Coconut Cream
50g / 2 oz Cashew Butter

2 Medjool Dates
1 ripe Banana
Ice cubes optional

Just blitz the lot in a blender until smooth. At half a litre it will keep in the fridge for 24 hours if you keep the banana out until you are ready to drink it, otherwise the banana causes the drink to go slimy and thick.

SWEET DELIGHTS

FRUIT SALAD

FRUIT SALAD

This really doesn't require much instruction. If you have never made a traditional fruit salad before, then simply take ripe, fresh fruit, varied in colour, texture and flavour, chop up and place in a bowl with a sprinkling of sugar and maybe a little fruit juice. Then leave covered at room temperature for about an hour.

Some of my favourite fruit salads are simple – made with three or four fruits, sugar, ground mixed spice and a squeeze of lime, they just sing!

Try being imaginative using things like pink grapefruit and fruit that is new to you. Adding nuts is also a lovely mix, especially toasted and slivered almonds.

And how about adding just a tablespoon of elderflower cordial. Especially lovely with sharp fruits.

COCONUT RICE PUDDING

COCONUT RICE PUDDING

One of my favourite comfort foods, hot in winter and chilled in summer. Great with jam or syrup of your choice.

Time: 2 hours. Oven 160°C. Serves 4

250ml Coconut Cream
600ml Soy Milk
80g / 3 oz Pudding Rice
25g / 1 oz Unsweetened Desiccated Coconut

25g / 1 oz Non-Dairy margarine for greasing dish
75g / 3 oz Sugar
Salt

1) Grease an oven-proof dish that has at least 900ml capacity.

2) Mix together in a jug the milk and the coconut cream.

3) Into the dish place the dry ingredients and then add the liquid.

4) Place in the centre of the oven and bake for 2 hours.

This pudding is a traditional favourite and it the one that has family members arguing over who has the skin! Well you can keep it, because the real beauty is what is underneath.

When you first peel back that bubbling golden top, you may find a very dense, slightly dry-looking pudding beneath. It is eaten like this by many, but I prefer to spoon out the contents minus the skin and transfer it into a saucepan and add extra milk or cream, warming it and stirring it to produce a really rich, velvety creaminess that is the best comfort food under the sun. That is how the pudding is represented in the image opposite.

Tip: For those wanting less calories and saturated fat, remove the coconut cream and replace with coconut milk.

ROASTED HAZELNUT & CHOCOLATE CHUNK COOKIES

Use any nut you like – pecans go well in this biscuit. Be generous with the chocolate chunks and the syrup, rice syrup being a possible replacement if you can't get golden.

Time: total 20 minutes. Oven 170°C. Makes 10–12

100g / 4 oz nuts of your choice (smashed but not pulverised)

85g / 3½ oz dark Solid Vegan Chocolate (broken into small chunks)

175g / 7 oz Self Raising Flour

100g / 4 oz Non-Dairy Margarine

Pinch coarse salt

4 generous dessert spoons of Golden Syrup (or Rice Syrup or other thick sweetener)

1 tablespoon Orange Juice

1 tablespoon Milk

1) Pre-heat the oven and put shelf in the middle.

2) Prep a large baking sheet with a layer of baking parchment.

3) Place all of the ingredients into a mixing bowl and mix together with a wooden spoon.

4) Once everything is really well mixed, sticky and slightly sloppy, scoop dessert-spoonfuls of mixture onto the baking tray parchment as neatly as you can. One spoonful equals one cookie. They will swell in size when they bake.

5) Once all of the mixture is spooned out then place the raw cookies in the oven for 10–12 minutes. They should just be going slightly golden and be slightly soft when you carefully remove them using a fish slice. Place on a cooling rack.

SPICED BASMATI RICE PUDDING
with Gooseberries in Elderflower Syrup

Time: Quick prep then 2 hours baking. Oven 160°C

500ml Sweetened Almond Milk
50g / 2 oz Basmati Rice (white)
25g / 1 oz Pudding Rice
40g / 1½ oz Sugar
1 tablespoon Vanilla Essence
Pinch of Salt
1 teaspoon Ground Mixed Spice

Non-Dairy Margarine to grease oven-proof dish
Fruit Accompaniment;
1 tablespoon Elderflower Cordial
200g Gooseberries
3–4 tablespoons Caster Sugar
3–4 tablespoons Water

1) Grease a litre / 2pint oven proof dish. Pre-heat oven.

2) Add all the rice pudding ingredients into the dish, milk last.

3) Leave dish uncovered and place on the middle shelf in the oven. This pudding does not need stirring or disturbing as it cooks.

4) Now prep the fruit. Wash the gooseberries and place in a saucepan with the sugar, water and cordial.

5) Gently heat so nothing burns, stirring occasionally and then once simmering, turn the heat down and allow the fruit to soften. Gooseberries change colour, yellowing slightly as they become soft. You want to catch them just as they start to do this, so they stay whole and not turn to mush and seeds. Using a slotted spoon remove them from the liquid and place in a bowl.

6) Now bring the liquid back up to the boil and simmer rapidly whilst stirring. This will help turn the liquid into a thin syrup. After a few minutes take off the heat and pour syrup over the gooseberries and allow to cool.

7) Once pudding has cooked, remove from the oven. It will have a skin on top where most of the mixed spice will have gathered. It is a thinner skin than with traditional rice pudding. I like to keep it with the rest of the rice, putting it all into a large saucepan and heating gently with extra cream, stirring continually to make the pudding smooth and creamy. Serve hot or cold with a spoonful of syrupy gooseberries.

It has a lovely Asian slant to the flavour from the Basmati rice, but still tastes like a rice pudding should. I am particularly proud of this culinary invention!

PINEAPPLE & RUM UPSIDE-DOWN CAKE

I never liked the classic upside-down cake, but this is light, sticky heaven.

Time: 50 minutes. Oven 160°C

- 100g / 4 oz Self Raising Flour
- 1 teaspoon Baking Powder
- 100g / 4 oz Non-Dairy Margarine
- 100g / 4 oz Caster Sugar
- 1½ teaspoons Rum Flavouring (or Rum if you have it)
- 3 teaspoons Ener-G Egg Replacer
- 4 tablespoons Orange Juice
- ½ fresh Pineapple
- 2 tablespoons Soft Brown Sugar
- 2 tablespoons Margarine for the base of tin for making the syrup topping
- 1 teaspoon Mixed Ground Spice or similar

1) Prepare the tin by lining it with parchment. Use a shallow sided tin. Remember to spread some margarine on the tin to make the parchment stick to it.

2) Now with at least 2 tablespoons of margarine, spread over the parchment on the base of the tin.

3) Now sprinkle the margarined base with the brown sugar and the ground spice. This will all caramelise with the pineapple to form a beautiful syrup.

4) Taking a half of a fresh pineapple, remove the skin and the inner core, and slice thinly. Lay the slices on the bottom of the tin on top of the sugar and spice, trying to form a complete layer. The slices can slightly over-lap.

5) Now turn on your oven to pre-heat while you make the sponge part.

6) In a mixing bowl cream together the margarine and the sugar with a whisk until light, but don't over-do it.

7) Sieve into the bowl the flour and baking powder but do not mix it up. Add the rum flavouring.

8) Now prepare the egg replacer by mixing the orange juice in with the Ener-G Egg Replacer powder in a jug, whisking with a fork or blender until frothy.

9) Add the egg mix to the mixing bowl and mix all together thoroughly.

10) Scrape out the mixture on top of the pineapple in the tin, spreading it carefully so that you form an even layer.

11) Bake on a middle shelf for 40 minutes.

12) Allow to cool for 5 minutes before placing a plate over the tin and with a tea towel (the tin with still be very hot), turn out the cake onto the plate. Unpeel the parchment to reveal the syrupy pineapple topping.

Eat hot with cream or custard. Keeps well for three days in the fridge.

STRAWBERRIES & CREAM TART

This is in three stages and quite time consuming as the yoghurt requires straining for 12 hours and the strawberry part needs chilling for 2 hours. But it is not technical as a dish. Is worth this effort as a centrepiece for a dinner party.

· Serves 12 easily

STRAWBERRIES & CREAM TART

- 1 Sweet Pastry Case, pre-made. (See 'Making Pastry' in the Skills Set section or buy one pre-made)
- 600g / 1 lb. 8 oz fresh Strawberries hulled and washed. Leave to drain on some kitchen paper.
- 500ml Strained Natural Soya Yoghurt (you will have started with 1 litre which after 12 hours will have halved in volume)
- 2 tablespoons Strawberry or Red Berry Cordial
- 50g / 2 oz Sugar
- Pinch of Salt
- 2½ tablespoons Agar Flakes / Powder

For Jelly Topping;
- 1 tablespoon Agar
- 250ml Pomegranate Juice (or other deep red juice)

1) Cut 500g / 1 lb 4 oz of the strawberries in half and lay them cut side down on some kitchen paper to soak up some of their moisture.

2) While the strawberries rest, put into a saucepan the cordial, sugar, agar, salt and all of the yoghurt.

3) Heat the contents of the pan gently, stirring continually, until it comes to the boil. Then turn the heat down and simmer gently, stirring. Do this for 6 – 8 minutes. This activates the agar which will set the yoghurt and strawberries.

4) Put the hot yoghurt mixture into a blender and add the resting strawberries to it. Blend until smooth.

5) Scoop all of the blended strawberry yoghurt mixture into the pastry case and even it out. When cool, place in a fridge and allow to set for around 2 hours.

6) Making the topping is very simple. Place the juice and agar into a pan and heat as you did before. Simmer for 6–8 minutes. When you add it to the top of the strawberry yoghurt do it a spoonful at a time, to prevent 'dimpling' the surface.

7) Allow the gel to set and refrigerate for 30 minutes.

Serve with the remaining strawberries and some single cream.

COCONUT, ORANGE & RASPBERRY CAKE

Coconut cake was something my Nan made, and it became a cake synonymous with Saturday tea-time. Here is my own take on the classic. Where my Nan used heaps of dairy butter, I use Orange and Raspberry to add the kick of wonderful flavour.

Time: 15 minutes prep, 1 hour baking. Oven 170–180°C

200g / 8 oz Self Raising Flour
1 teaspoon Baking Powder
100g / 4 oz Non-Dairy Margarine
100g / 4 oz Soft Brown Sugar
50g / 2 oz Desiccated Coconut (unsweetened)

Juice and Zest of 1 Large Orange
Handful of fresh Raspberries (12 – 15)
3 teaspoons Ener-G Egg Replacer
4 tablespoons carton Orange Juice

1) Prepare a high sided, loose bottomed 7–8" cake tin by greasing with margarine and lining with parchment. (See the 'Skills Set' section, page 28, if you are not sure how to do this.)

2) In a large mixing bowl sift the flour and baking powder, add the salt and the margarine. Rub the margarine into the flour with your fingertips until it resembles bread crumbs.

3) Now add the coconut, sugar and orange zest and mix together.

4) Wait until the oven is at the required temperature and the shelf is in the middle position before doing the next steps, since the cake must go immediately into the oven once you have levelled the mixture.

5) Add the fresh orange juice to the dry mixture. Make sure your raspberries are ready and NOT dripping wet from rinsing them. Dry them with some paper towel.

6) Place the egg replacing powders into a small blender or into a jug and add the carton orange juice. Blend or whisk until well mixed and immediately pour into the cake mixture.

7) Now stir quickly and thoroughly with a wooden spoon.

8) Put roughly half the mixture into the tin and very rapidly level it out to the edges of the tin. Now sprinkle the raspberries over it and press them down into the mixture with your hand.

9) Now quickly pour and scrape the rest of the mixture over the top of the raspberries taking care to smother them and level the cake mixture roughly.

10) NOW GET IT IN THE OVEN!

11) Bake for 55–60 minutes then check with a skewer or thin knife to see if cooked through. Do this by inserting the skewer or knife into three places down to the tin's base and if it comes out clean then the cake is done. Remember the raspberries will be wet, but the cake should not be.

12) Allow cake to cool for 5 minutes before removing from tin. Place the tin on top of a teacup and gently push the sides of the tin down to reveal the cake. Lift the cake up using a tea towel and place on a cooling rack. Remove the tin base using a fish slice, once the cake is cooled.

COCONUT, ORANGE & RASPBERRY CAKE

DOUBLE CHOCOLATE & PECAN 'BROWNIE' BISCUITS

A cross between a chocolate brownie and a cookie, so hence the name. As satisfying as a chocolate cake but much quicker to make!

Time: 20 minutes in total. Oven 170°C. Makes 10–12

- 100g / 4 oz Pecans (smashed, but not pulverised)
- 80g / 3½ oz dark solid Vegan Chocolate (broken into small chunks)
- 150g / 6 oz Self raising Flour
- 25g / 1 oz Raw Cacao Powder
- 100g / 4 oz Non-Dairy Margarine
- Pinch coarse Salt
- 4 generous dessert-spoonfuls of Golden or Maple Syrup
- 3–4 tablespoons of Milk
- 1 tablespoon Orange Juice

1) Pre-heat oven and place shelf in the middle.

2) Prep a large baking sheet with a layer of baking parchment.

3) Place all of the ingredients into a mixing bowl and using a wooden spoon, mix thoroughly together. This should produce a sticky, slightly sloppy mix.

4) Spoon the mixture a dessert-spoonful at a time onto the baking tray parchment, leaving a little space between each, as they will swell slightly whilst baking. If making 10–12 cookies, bake for 8–10 minutes. If making 6–8 larger ones, bake for 12 minutes.

5) When cooked remove immediately and lift gently from tray with a fish slice, onto a cooling rack. They will still be soft so take care, until they are cool.

DOUBLE CHOCOLATE & PECAN 'BROWNIE' BISCUITS

CHOCOLATE & CASHEW BUTTER MOUSSE

CHOCOLATE & CASHEW BUTTER MOUSSE

The longer you chill this, the better it gets. It will blow everyone away who tries it because it tastes too creamy and rich to be vegan – so everyone else says!

Time: 20 minutes prep, 1 hour chill. Makes 3–4 servings

180g / 7 oz Firm Silken Tofu (pressed for ½ hour)
85g / 3–4 oz Plain Vegan Chocolate
¼ cup Smooth Roasted Cashew Butter
140ml / ½ a pack Rice Whipping Cream

2 tablespoon Agave Nectar / other honey substitute
pinch salt
Orange zest to decorate.

1) Press Tofu (see 'Skills Set' page)

2) Whilst Tofu is being pressed take a small bowl and break up chocolate into it and melt it by placing the bowl into a pan of hot water. Heat gently.

3) Once fully melted, take the pan off the heat and add to the bowl the salt, agave and cashew butter. Stir to allow to mix and soften slightly.

4) In a separate small bowl place the rice whipping cream and whip with hand whisk for 2 minutes until very light.

5) Take pressed tofu and place in a blender/processor and blitz a little. Then add the chocolate mixture and blitz until smooth. Keep stopping and scraping mixture off the sides to get everything mixed well.

6) Once smooth, fold in the whipped cream gently until everything is well mixed and the colour is even, without streaks.

7) Spoon into serving dishes and chill for an hour for best results.

8) Decorate with a little grated orange zest.

RASPBERRY FRANGIPANE

I adore anything flavoured with almond, so frangipane, best known to me as Bakewell Tart, is a real favourite. This is my own version of a British classic.

Time: 30 minutes prep, 40 minutes baking time. Oven 170°C

Pastry

125g / 5 oz Plain Flour
50g / 2 oz Cornflour
85–90g / 3½ oz Non-Dairy Margarine
3 tablespoons cold water

Pinch Salt
25g / 1 oz Caster Sugar
Zest of one lemon

Filling (Frangipane)

100g / 4 oz Non-Dairy Margarine
100g / 4 oz Agave Nectar / Sweet Freedom
140g / 5½ oz Finely Ground Almonds
100g / 4 oz Self Raising Flour
Pinch Salt

3 teaspoons Ener-G Egg Replacer
4 tablespoons Orange Juice
2 tablespoons Lemon Juice
1½ teaspoons Almond Extract

Other

2–4 tablespoons seedless Raspberry Jam and fresh Raspberries

1) Prepare the pastry first and line the flan tin. See Skills Set section for this (page 28). Add the extra ingredient of lemon zest when you add the sugar and the cornflour simply gets mixed with the plain flour.

2) Once your pastry is in the tin, spoon on the raspberry jam and spread all over the base. Chill the pastry-lined tin for 30 minutes.

3) Place the margarine and agave into a mixing bowl and cream together. They may appear to split but do not worry.

4) Add all of the other ingredients except the Ener-G powder and the orange juice. Mix roughly but do not try to mix all together. It is too dry at this point.

5) Now add the orange juice to the Ener-G powder and whisk together until frothy.

6) Add the egg replacer to the mixing bowl and now with a wooden spoon mix together thoroughly. You should have a paste which seems textured and soft enough to dollop of a spoon with a little encouragement. If yours is completely stuck to the spoon and won't budge add a little more orange juice or milk.

7) Now scoop out all the mixture into the pastry case, levelling it out as much as possible. Take your handful of raspberries and push them individually into the mixture about half way.

8) Bake on the middle shelf for 40 minutes. You will need to cover it with foil or parchment halfway through to avoid the frangipane drying out or burning.

This is wonderful hot with cream or custard, or left to cool and eaten as is with a cup of tea. Also good with a little drizzle of lemon icing.

RASPBERRY FRANGIPANE

CITRUS 'CHEESECAKE'
with Blackcurrant or Fruit Juice Topping

CITRUS 'CHEESECAKE'

Very easy to do, but takes some prior preparation of two ingredients: the nuts (4–6 hours) and the yoghurt (strained overnight).

Time: Prep 30 minutes; prep yoghurt & nuts in advance. Chill for a minimum of 4 hours

Base:

- 8 Ginger Snap Biscuits (my supermarket's own brand is vegan)
- 2 tablespoons Non-Dairy Margarine
- 1 heaped tablespoon Golden Syrup
- 75g / ¾ cup Rolled Oats
- Pinch of Salt

Cheesecake centre:

- 1 litre Plain Soya (or Coconut or Almond) Yogurt strained overnight and then in a bowl of paper towel in the fridge for a morning
- 1½ cup Plain Cashews soaked for 4–6 hours in water
- ½–¾ cup Icing Sugar

ROOTED: RECIPES

2 tablespoons Vegetable or Nut Oil

1 tablespoon Lemon Extract (plus 1 teaspoon Orange Extract if you have it)

1 tablespoon Vanilla Extract

Juice ½ Lime

1½ tablespoons Agar Flakes / Powder (If you wish to make this raw, then do not use Agar and omit stage 7 and 8)

¼ teaspoon Salt

Toppings:

150g / 6 oz Blackcurrants

2 tablespoons Soft Brown Sugar

Pinch of Salt

OR

300ml Orange or Tropical Juice

1 teaspoon Orange Extract

1 tablespoon Agar flakes

1) Prepare the yogurt as described in the Skill Set section 'Straining Yoghurt' (page 39). Put nuts in a bowl and generously fill with boiling water. Cover and leave at room temperature for 4–6 hours. Drain and rinse and keep in air tight container until using. You could of course soak the nuts overnight along with the yoghurt.

2) You will need a 6–7" high sided spring-form tin.

3) Crush the ginger biscuits in a bowl. I do this with the end of my rolling pin. Then add the oats to them.

4) Melt the margarine in a small saucepan and take off the heat. Add to it the syrup and salt. Mix together until all melted together but don't re-heat. Now add to the dry ingredients and stir well.

5) Tip all of the ginger oat mixture into the bottom of the tin, and spread evenly right up to the tin's edges. Firm down with the back of a spoon or with the back of your fingers. Now chill while you prepare the rest of the cake.

6) Place the nuts in a food processor (fitted with S blade) and blitz until well broken and mixed together. Add with it the icing sugar, the extracts, half the yoghurt and the oil. Blend this until entirely smooth, or as smooth as your processor will allow.

7) In a small non-stick pan place the remaining half of the yoghurt and add to it the salt and the agar flakes.

8) Gently warm this mixture and stir as you do so. You need to bring it to boiling and then simmer for 8 minutes to activate the agar and make sure it is properly dissolved. Once this is done, transfer all of it to the blender with the other ingredients and blend together. You need to taste test and add any further sweetener or extracts to your liking.

9) You can now transfer all of this mixture into the tin on top of the ginger oat base. Smooth it evenly and then chill for three hours minimum. Four hours is even better and leaving it twelve will perfect it. (If you haven't used agar you will need to leave it overnight.)

10) The toppings are simple to make. For the blackcurrant topping, place the blackcurrants and sugar in a saucepan with a tablespoon of water and a pinch of salt, bring to the boil and rapidly simmer for several minutes. Then place the blackcurrant sauce in a small jug or bowl and allow to cool. I spoon it over the cake when I am ready to serve and chill it for 20 minutes to allow it to settle. But it is rather nice having it dribble over the edges as you cut a slice.

11) The fruit juice gel is made by heating the juice with the agar in a pan until boiling, and simmering for 6–8 minutes. Then spoon the liquid onto the cheesecake and it sets as it cools. Chill.

BLACKCURRANT 'CHEESECAKE'

SPICED FRUIT TEA LOAF

I adore spice and fruit together and this tea loaf is such a treat, warm with butter (vegan of course) and accompanied with a cup of Earl Grey tea.

Time: this needs proving for 2 hours and cooking for 25 minutes. Oven 200°C top shelf

7g / 1½ teaspoons Active Dried Yeast

270ml warmed Almond or Mild Soya Milk (or half water half milk)

1 teaspoon Caster Sugar

1 cup Mixed Dried Fruit

500g White Bread Flour (or ⅔ white with ⅓ malt flour)

1 teaspoon Salt

3 teaspoons Vegetable Oil

1½ tablespoons Soft Brown Sugar

1–2 teaspoons Ground Mixed Spice

1) Prepare the yeast: in warm milk put the yeast and teaspoon of sugar, and whisk. Put a saucer on top and leave in a warm spot for 15 minutes or until 1 cm froth has built up. If froth doesn't show then the milk is either too hot, too cold or the yeast is old. Discard and start again.

2) In a large mixing bowl place all of the other ingredients and mix together.

3) Once yeast is ready, whisk again and add it to the dry ingredients

4) Mix together until all of the liquid is soaked up.

5) Tip out the mixture and squeeze together to form a rough ball. Then begin to knead.

6) Kneading stretches the protein fibres and makes the dough 'elastic' so that is can expand with the gasses produced by the yeast. You need to knead the dough around 10 minutes for best results. Rhythmically push one side of the dough into the middle then the other side, pushing the dough down with the heel of your hand. It is quite an effort if you are not used to it.

7) Once the dough is kneaded and feels soft and stretchy, place it into a large bread tin (or two smaller ones) which have been greased. Fruit bread tends to stick to my non-stick bread tins for some reason!

8) Now pop in a warm place with a damp cloth over them but not touching. If the cloth touches the dough as it rises, it will stick and removing it will tear a hole in the surface causing a big sagging dip. Fashion a scaffold using bottles on a baking tray.

9) Allow to rise for 2 hours. The dough should triple in size at least.

10) Make sure the oven is at its correct temperature before putting the bread into it. Allow to cook for 20–30 minutes depending on whether it is one tin or two smaller tins.

11) Tip the loaf immediately out of its tin. It is cooked when brown on top and sounds hollow when you tap the bottom of the loaf.

Tip: Cool on a rack. It is nice warm, but do not slice it until it has cooled for 20 minutes minimum, or the bread might not cut cleanly.

LEMON SPONGE TRAY BAKE

Time: 15 minutes prep, 30 minutes baking. Oven 170°C, middle shelf

100g Non-Dairy Margarine

100g Caster Sugar

1 tablespoon Agave Nectar

150g Self Raising Flour (sieved with) 50g Cornflour, and 2 teaspoons Baking Powder and 1 teaspoon Baking Soda

1 Lemon juiced plus Zest of 1 Lemon (or add orange zest for a bitter twist)

Pinch of Salt

4½ teaspoons Ener-G Egg Replacer

90 ml / 6 tablespoons of Orange Juice

Couple of drops of Lemon Extract

With any cake mix involving a powdered egg replacer and baking soda/powder, it is essential that the moment these items touch liquid they go straight into the oven. They begin to work once they are mixed, so preparation is key.

1) Prepare the baking tray (a high sided roughly 24cm square tin) by lining with parchment. If you smear the tin with margarine first the parchment will easily stick to the sides and you can push and fold the corners in neatly. Do this even if your tin is a non-stick type. The sponge will be fragile when it comes out of the oven and lifting it out using the parchment will stop it cracking apart, especially if you are serving it hot.

2) Prepare the egg replacer by measuring out the powder and placing it into a small blender or jug. Have the water measured ready but DO NOT add to the powder yet.

3) Put your oven on making sure the shelf is in the middle.

4) In a large mixing bowl place the margarine and the sugar and cream together with a spoon. As it softens use a manual hand whisk to feather it up so it becomes light but do not over-do this. A minute or two is plenty.

5) Now add the agave to the margarine and sugar and beat that in with the whisk. Remove as much mixture from the whisk as you can when done.

6) Now sieve the flours, baking powder and soda into the bowl, and add the zest and salt. Don't mix just yet.

7) Go to your egg replacer and add the orange juice. Blend, either electrically or with a fork, until the water and powder are well blended and frothing slightly.

8) Now add the egg replacer liquid AND the lemon juice and extract to the mixing bowl and stir together rapidly and thoroughly. Immediately transfer this mixture to the prepared tin, level out with the back of the spoon very roughly and get into the oven.

LEMON SPONGE TRAY BAKE

9) Bake for 25–30 minutes. Check it is cooked by popping a skewer or thin knife into the cake in three different places. If it comes out clean it is cooked.

This sponge does not rise a lot, so keeps its moisture and density. Is delicious with custard , especially if you smear some raspberry jam on top, or can be cooled and sandwiched together with cream and jam. To do this I just make the one tin, cut the square in half and then sandwich the two halves making an attractive rectangular sponge cake.

Tip: To make a cream filling use 50g / 2oz margarine and icing sugar and mix together. You could use coconut crème or rice whipping cream as an alternative, but make sure these are well chilled before use.

PEANUT BUTTER & BANANA OATIE

PEANUT BUTTER & BANANA OATIE

Time: Prep and cook total 40 minutes. Oven 150°C, 20–25 mins, middle shelf. Makes 12–18 oaties

700g / 7 cups Rolled Porridge Oats
175g Non-Dairy Margarine
280g Golden or Maple Syrup
180g Unsalted Smooth Peanut Butter (or Cashew Butter)

2 ripe Bananas, mashed
1 cup / 2 handfuls Mixed Dried Fruit
Juice and zest of 1 Lemon
½ teaspoon Coarse Salt

1) Gently melt the margarine, sugar and syrup in a saucepan just enough to warm through. It must not get too hot or starts to burn.

2) Put all the dry ingredients (including banana if using) and the lemon juice into a large mixing bowl.

3) Add the warm peanut butter mixture into the dry ingredients and mix thoroughly together.

4) Now follow the instructions in the Skill Set section on how to Prepare Oaties for the Oven.

5) Bake until golden brown all over. Cool and cut into squares whilst still in the tin. (That is highly unlikely in our house!)

SWEET DELIGHTS

ALMOND & COCONUT BISCUITS

ALMOND & COCONUT BISCUITS

Very quick, thin and delicious, melt-in-the-mouth treats that everyone seems to love.

Time: 20 minutes to make and bake. Oven 170°C. Makes 20–22 biscuits

Ingredients;
- 100g / 4 oz Self Raising Flour
- 50g / 2 oz Ground Almonds
- 50g / 2 oz Desiccated Coconut
- 50g / 2 oz Soft Brown Sugar
- 100g / 4 oz Non-Dairy Margarine
- ½ teaspoon Almond Essence
- Pinch of Salt
- Vegan Chocolate to decorate

1) Prepare a baking sheet with parchment and pre-heat the oven, putting the oven tray in the middle.

2) Place all the ingredients into a mixing bowl and stir together with a wooden spoon. This should produce a thick, almost paste-like consistency, very soft to touch.

3) Once everything is thoroughly blended, turn out onto a well-floured surface and gently roll with a pin. The dough is very soft so no need to press down, just let the weight of the pin do the work, and keep the dough moving or it will stick to the table.

4) Once you have it to a point where you can handle the dough gently (this may take several sprinklings of extra flour), then you can cut out the biscuit rounds. Make the biscuits as thin as you can without them falling apart. This takes a bit of practise but is worth the effort.

5) Place the biscuits on the tray and bake for 10–12 minutes. Remove immediately from tray and place on a cooling rack. When cool, drizzle melted chocolate over them or any icing/decoration you prefer.

CASHEW & COFFEE MOUSSE

Light and luscious!

Time: Tofu needs pressing for 3 hours and the dessert needs chilling for a minimum of an hour

- 360g / 14–15 oz pack of Firm Silken Tofu pressed for 3 hours
- 350g / 14 oz pack of Rice Whipping Cream chilled in the fridge to firm
- 180g / 7½ oz Roasted Cashew Butter (or unroasted)
- 6 tablespoons Icing Sugar (or more if you prefer)
- ¼ teaspoon Salt
- 1 tablespoon Coffee Extract
- 2 tablespoons Raw Cacao Powder
- 2 tablespoons Soft Brown Sugar
- 1 teaspoon Coffee granules in 1 teaspoon hot water
- OR 1 tablespoon freshly brewed filter coffee

1) Press the Tofu for three hours as instructed in the Skills Set Section (page 38).

2) Once pressed, place Tofu and all other ingredients into a blender or processor and blend until perfectly smooth. You will need to keep stopping the processor and scraping down the sides.

3) Place the mixture into serving dishes (I like using tea or coffee cups) and chill in the fridge for a minimum of an hour. Gets better the longer it is left in the fridge.

Lovely served with almond or ginger biscuits.

Tip: If you can't get hold of Rice Whipping Cream, then you can order it online or use Coconut Cream instead – but you must chill this for a couple of days to firm it up enough. Don't use coconut milk as this is too runny.

CASHEW & COFFEE MOUSSE

RASPBERRY SYLLABUB

RASPBERRY SYLLABUB

Time: 20 minutes prep and then chill time – the longer the better

200g fresh Raspberries (if washed these must be drained and dried with some kitchen paper)

4 tablespoons Icing Sugar

450g Rice Whipping Cream

The easiest dessert to make and one of the most refreshing. Take the raspberries and half the icing sugar and blitz together until smooth. Using a blender should blitz the pips too.

Now in a separate bowl whip the cream and the remaining icing sugar together for two minutes to lighten and increase its volume.

Now fold the raspberries carefully into the cream until it is thoroughly mixed. Spoon into dessert dishes or glasses and chill for as long as you can. They get better the longer they are left.

Tip: Also lovely as a topping on bananas, tofu or yoghurt tarts and with thin almond biscuits.

CELEBRATION / CHRISTMAS CAKE

Time: 30 mins, prep 2 hours baking plus optional month of drizzling liquor into cake. Oven 140°C

- 150g / 6 oz Non-Dairy Margarine
- 150g / 6 oz Soft Brown Sugar
- 12 / 5–6 oz Soaked Prunes
- 250g / 10 oz Mixed Dried Fruit and Peel (Must be fresh – not old dried out fruit or this will give you a dried out cake – if the fruit seems a little hard, try soaking for 4 hours in boiling water)
- 3 ripe Figs or dried figs that have been soaked
- 5 fl. oz Orange Juice
- 3 fl. oz Ruby Port or Brandy
- ¼ teaspoon Salt
- 1 cup crushed Pecans or Walnuts
- Zest of 1 Orange
- 2½ tablespoons Ground Mixed Spice
- 2 teaspoons Baking Powder
- 3 teaspoons Ener-G Egg Replacer with 4 tablespoons orange juice BUT DO NOT ADD TOGETHER YET
- 12 oz Self Raising Flour
- Optional extra 'booze' to drizzle onto cake and allow to soak in plus marzipan and soft icing to decorate. These can be pre-made. May need to check if they are vegan. Also some marmalade or apricot jam to use as the 'glue' between cake and marzipan, and marzipan and icing.

1) Place the margarine, sugar, prunes, mixed dried fruit, pecans, figs, orange juice, alcohol and salt into a saucepan and warm together gently to avoid burning.

2) Bring to the boil slowly, stirring occasionally and then turn heat down low and allow to simmer gently with a lid on, for about 20 minutes. Stir once or twice during this time.

3) After twenty minutes pour all the saucepan's contents into a mixing bowl and allow to stand and cool for around 30 minutes. Cover with a tea towel or something loose to allow some of the water to evaporate.

4) Prepare a high sided loose bottomed 7–8" cake tin by lining it. (See Skills Set section 'Lining Tins', page 42, for help with this).

5) Once your fruit and sugar mix has cooled off for the half hour, add the flour, zest, baking powder, and mixed spice, BUT DO NOT STIR YET.

6) Now prepare the egg replacer by adding the orange juice to it and whisking with a fork or a blender until frothy.

7) Add the egg replacer to everything else and mix with a wooden spoon very thoroughly. It should produce a heavy, cloggy cake mix, not too soft or too thick. Scrape it all into the cake tin and roughly level it out to reach the tin's edges.

CELEBRATION / CHRISTMAS CAKE

8) Cover the tin with some foil and bake in the oven, low to middle shelf, for 2 hours.

9) Once it is cooled completely you can prick with a cocktail stick in several places and add a drizzle of brandy or rum into the cake to further enrich the flavour over the next few weeks, as long as you keep it in an air-tight container.

CARROT CAKE TRAY BAKE
with Cashew Butter & Tofu Frosting

Time: 10 minutes prep, 40 baking time. Oven middle shelf 170°C

CARROT CAKE TRAY BAKE

- 180g Carrot, peeled and finely grated (lace between sheets of kitchen paper to pat excess moisture away)
- 180g Mashed Ripe Banana
- ½ cup crushed Pecans
- 220g Self Raising Flour
- 160g Soft Brown Sugar
- ⅓ cup Vegetable Oil
- 1½ teaspoons Baking Soda
- 1 teaspoon Baking Powder
- 3 measures Ener-G Egg Replacer (4½ teaspoons powder with 6 tablespoons water)
- 1 teaspoon Ground Mixed Spice
- Pinch of Salt

Topping

360g Firm Silken Tofu (requires pressing to provide around 220g of denser Tofu)

Pinch of Salt

½ Lemon juiced

1 cup Icing Sugar

2 tablespoons Non-Dairy Cream

1 tablespoon Roasted Cashew Butter (½ tablespoon smooth Peanut Butter will do)

1) Line the base of a square tray bake tin, roughly 24–26cm across. (This sort of tin has higher sides than a baking tray)

2) In a large mixing bowl place all of the dry ingredients first. Mix with a spoon. This includes the carrot and the banana.

3) Now add the oil.

4) Put the Ener-G Powder and water into a small blender (or a bowl and use a hand blender) and whiz together until foamy. **Do not do this part until the oven is ready,** as once this egg replacer is mixed it begins to work and needs to be mixed with the cake mixture and put in the oven as quickly as possible. The water will also activate the Baking Soda and Powder.

5) Add the Ener-G liquid into the bowl and mix quickly and thoroughly. Tip all of it into the tin and spread out quickly. It doesn't have to be perfect, just roughly level.

6) Put tin immediately in the oven and leave to bake for at least 30 minutes. Look to see if it is golden. If not, leave for another ten minutes. Then check to see if the centre is cooked by putting a skewer or slim knife into it. If it comes out clean it is cooked.

7) Allow the cake to cool completely before you add the frosting. The frosting can be made now and refrigerated until needed.

8) To make the frosting simply place all of the ingredients into a blender and whiz until smooth. When needed spread it over the top of the cake in a nice generous layer. Chill the cake and keep it chilled for best results.

Tip: If you don't like to use Tofu you could use vegan soft cheese, strained yoghurt or Rice Whipping Cream. Whip this up with a whisk for at least 2 minutes before folding in the other ingredients.

Tip: I have found that baking this in a traditional round high-sided cake tin is not so successful – there is a tendency for it to sink.

RUM & CHOCOLATE TART
on a Ginger Oat Base

This is a quick 30 minute pudding once you have strained the yoghurt which takes 12 hours (overnight).

Makes one 6–7" tart requiring high-sided, spring form tin

500ml strained Plain Soya Yoghurt (you will need 1 litre to start with, so two 500ml tubs – see the 'Skill Set' section, page 39)

2 tablespoons nut oil – I use Almond Oil

1 tablespoon Cashew Butter (Roasted or unroasted)

8 tablespoons Raw Cacao Powder

Pinch of Salt

100g Caster Sugar

2 tablespoon Non-Dairy Margarine

2½ tablespoons Agar flakes / powder

2 tablespoons Rum flavouring

1 cup / 240ml mild Soya Milk or Oat Milk

For the base:

8 Vegan Ginger Snap biscuits

2 tablespoons Non-Dairy Margarine

1–2 tablespoons honey substitute (as thick as you can find – Sweet Freedom is good for this or Golden Syrup)

1 cup Rolled Porridge Oats

For the Topping

Making the topping that is in the photo simply requires a box of rice or coconut whipping cream which is vegan. If this is not available in your supermarket (it isn't in mine) then it can be ordered online.

Coconut cream (not coconut whipping cream) can be used as the topping if it has been refrigerated for about a week as it stiffens when very chilled.

Eating this tart with single cream is just as delectable.

1) Place the ginger biscuits in a plastic bag or inside a tea towel, and bash with a rolling pin. Don't blitz them in a processor or they go to dust. It is better to have a grittier texture.

2) Place the crushed biscuits into a bowl and add the oats. Put to one side.

3) Warm the honey substitute and margarine in a water bath (in a bowl which sits in a saucepan of warm water) and allow them to melt and stir together.

4) Once melted, add to it the crushed biscuit and oat mixture and stir thoroughly making sure all of the oats get coated with the liquid.

RUM & CHOCOLATE TART

5) If you haven't already, grease your tin with some margarine, and line with parchment, both the base and the sides. (See the 'Skills Set' section, page 42, if you are not sure how to do this).

6) Now tip in the ginger oat mixture and press firmly down, making sure it is level and goes right to the edges. Now pop this tin in the fridge to chill while you prepare the filling.

7) In a large jug or high-sided bowl, place the strained yoghurt, oil and cashew butter and whisk together to blend well. It is a good idea to use a hand blender or electric whisk. Place to the side.

8) In a non-stick pan place the raw cacao, salt, sugar, margarine, agar, rum flavouring and milk, and with a hand whisk on a low heat blend together with a steady figure of eight motion.

9) Once the ingredients seems to be blended, turn up the heat a little and bring the whole thing to the boil.

10) Once boiling, turn down the heat to a gentle simmer, so it is just bubbling slightly, and stir continually for 8 minutes. This ensures the agar is properly dissolved and activated.

11) After the 8 minutes, remove from the heat and add to the jug with the yoghurt and cashew butter. Mix thoroughly together. Spoon mixture into the chilled tin with the biscuit base.

12) Level off the chocolate rum mixture with a spatula or spoon, and allow to cool in the room. Once cool then place in the fridge to properly set. This takes around 2 hours.

Tip: A word of advice at this point. Whips and tarts that I make ALWAYS improve with at least 12 hours in the fridge. It will be tempting to cut into it before that, but results are far better when the tart has settled and properly solidified.

Tip: Whipping creams can sometimes be a bit runny or soft, and can be affected by warmth. If this happens whip it in a bowl and chill for an hour. Then spoon it onto your dessert and chill again for as long as you can stand it before cutting into it.

PEANUT BUTTER OATIE

Time: 40 minutes total. Oven 160°C 20–25 minutes. Makes 12–18 Oaties

5 cups Rolled Porridge Oats (or substitute 1 cup for Ground Flax or similar)

1 cup Mixed Dried Fruit

1 cup chopped Figs, Prunes or Dates

2 cups (300g) unsalted Smooth Peanut Butter

100g Non-Dairy Margarine

¾ cup honey substitute (Agave Nectar or Sweet Freedom)

2 tablespoons Vegetable Oil

Zest of 1 lemon

1) Place the margarine, honey substitute and vegetable oil into a saucepan and gently warm to melt together. Take off the heat and add the peanut butter, being patient and letting the warmth of the liquid soften the peanut butter. Don't heat as it easily burns.

2) In a large mixing bowl put all the other ingredients and mix together.

3) Now add the warm peanut butter mixture and mix thoroughly together. This will take a bit of time to make sure all the oats are coated and the fruit evenly distributed.

4) On a baking tray, maximum 38cm x 26cm, and lined with parchment/baking paper, tip all of the mixture and roughly distribute it across the whole tin, right into the corners.

5) Now follow the instructions in the Skill Set section on 'Preparing Oaties for the Oven', page 36.

6) Bake on the middle shelf until golden all over.

Allow to cool and cut it into pieces whilst still in the tin as this helps it hold together better.

Keep in an airtight container to retain moisture and these will last up to ten days, although that is highly unlikely in our house!

CRISPY NUT & ORANGE OATIE

Time: 20 minutes prep, 25 minutes cooking. Oven 160°C middle shelf. Makes 18 Oatie squares

3 cups slightly blitzed Rolled Oats

3 cups of Toasted Rice Cereal (unsweetened)

½ cup partially blitzed Pistachios

½ cup Golden Flax Seed

1 cup Mixed Dried Fruit (or dried fruit of your choice)

½ cup Agave Nectar or other vegan sweetener

100g / 4 oz Non-Dairy Margarine

½ cup smooth unsalted Peanut Butter

Juice of half an Orange and Zest of whole Orange

Generous pinch of Sea Salt

1) You will need a large baking tray/sheet (maximum 26 x 38cm) and a piece of baking parchment big enough to cover it plus an extra piece for pressing down mixture.

2) Into a saucepan place the margarine, peanut butter, honey substitute, orange juice and zest, and salt, and gently warm through to melt together – but do not overheat or it will burn. You only want it to mix together and warmth is enough.

3) In a large mixing bowl put all the other ingredients in and mix together.

4) Add the warm ingredients to the mixing bowl and with a wooden spoon mix everything well. This may take a little time. At first you may think it too dry – but it won't be.

5) When it is fully mixed, tip it all into the lined baking tray/sheet, and spread evenly around right into the corners. Press down the mixture firstly with the back of a spoon or a spatula. Now follow the instruction in the Skill Set section on 'Preparing Oaties for the Oven' (page 36).

6) Bake on middle shelf until golden all over.

7) When done, allow to cool almost cold IN THE TIN and cut it into pieces whilst still in the tin as this helps it hold together better.

8) Store in airtight container. These keep for weeks, but they won't last that long!

Tip: If peanut butter is a no-no for you, try using pressed tofu, one ripe banana or ½ cup apple sauce instead. Add more salt too.

SWEET DELIGHTS

CHERRY BRANDY CHOCOLATE WHIP

Time: 30–40 minutes prep then 2 hours chilling minimum

For the Whip

- 85g of Plain Vegan Chocolate
- 360g Firm Silken Tofu (pressed to give approx. 220g)
- 2 tablespoons Non-Dairy Single Cream
- 2 tablespoons Non-Dairy Margarine
- 2 tablespoons Honey Substitute
- 2 tablespoons Vegan Cherry Brandy
- Pinch sea salt

For the Cherry Sauce

- 10–12 ripe Red or Black Cherries
- 2 tablespoons Vegan Cherry Cordial
- ⅓ cup Soft Brown Sugar (or Sweet Freedom)
- 1 tablespoon Non-Dairy Margarine
- Pinch salt
- Pinch of Arrowroot powder or ¼ teaspoon cornflour (use the end of a teaspoon handle)

1) Press the Tofu; see Skill Set section (page 38). Whilst Tofu is being pressed you can prepare the rest of the ingredients

2) Using a water bath (a bowl inside a saucepan of water), place the chocolate broken into pieces, margarine, fruit honey, brandy and salt and gently warm, stirring occasionally. Once almost fully melted together, remove bowl from heat and stir until smooth. Leave to cool a little.

3) Put the pressed tofu into a food processor and blitz slightly to break up. Then add the melted chocolate mixture and blend until smooth. You will have to keep stopping the processor and scraping the mixture down off the sides of the bowl so all ingredients is thoroughly blended.

4) Add the cream and blitz again until mixed thoroughly.

5) Spoon the whip into dessert dishes and place in fridge to chill.

6) About 20 minutes before serving, make the cherry sauce. Take the cherries, wash and cut open to stone them. Chop into smaller pieces. You may wish to blitz them to make a different texture sauce. I tend to cut into quarters as the added texture contrasts nicely with the silky whip.

7) In a non-stick pan place the margarine, cherry brandy, sugar, salt, arrowroot and cherries.

8) Very gently heat, stirring continually with a wooden spoon. Once sugar has dissolved, turn up the heat a little and get the liquid to boiling point, continually stirring.

9) Once boiling turn the heat down a little and keep stirring until the sauce starts to thicken. Then remove from heat. The sauce will begin to solidify straight away so you need to spoon it onto the desserts immediately.

MOIST FRUIT CAKE

MOIST FRUIT CAKE

Time: 30 minutes prep, 30 minutes cooling, 1 hour cooking. Oven 150–160°C middle shelf

250g / 10 oz Mixed Dried Fruit

2 small Eating Apples, diced, with skins left on

50g / 2 oz Soft Brown Sugar plus 50g / 2 oz Agave Nectar

100g / 4 oz Non-Dairy Margarine

150ml / ¼ pint fruit juice (freshly squeezed is best)

Zest of orange or lemon

pinch of Salt

200g / 8 oz Self Raising Flour plus 1 teaspoon Baking Powder

1 ½ tablespoons Ground Mixed Spice

1 egg worth of Ener-G Egg Replacer (see directions on packet)

Optional handful of Chopped Nuts, Cherries or Seeds.

Optional dash of Sloe Gin or other.

1) Line a loaf tin or high sided cake tin with baking parchment (see Skills Set, page 42).

2) Take the dried fruit, apples, sugar, margarine, zest and fruit juice and place in a saucepan and very gently heat, so the margarine melts. Stir well and heat gently until the mixture begins to bubble.

3) Turn heat right down so that the sugar does not burn, and let it simmer on lowest heat for about 20 minutes. Do this with the lid on.

4) Remove from heat and pour contents of pan into a bowl to cool. Leave for at least 30 minutes.

5) Place all other ingredients into a large mixing bowl. Add the wet ingredients that has cooled and stir quickly. This mixture needs to be put into its tin immediately as it will thicken and foam slightly. Get into a pre-heated oven and bake for 55–60 minutes on the middle shelf.

6) Push a slim knife into cake to check it is cooked. Knife should come out clean. Allow to cool for five minutes before removing from tin by lifting it out by the parchment paper if you can.

7) Allow to cool thoroughly on a wire rack before cutting.

Tip: Like most cakes this is best the next day – if you can wait that long!

JAM ROLY POLY

A British favourite and rightly so. No comfort food like it on a cold, drizzly night.

Time: 15 minutes prep, 30 mins cooking. Oven 190°C middle shelf

1 cup Self Raising Flour
½ cup Vegetable Suet
⅓ cup cold Water

Pinch of good Salt
Jam of your choice (raspberry is really good)

1) Add all the ingredients except the jam, into a mixing bowl, and stir together with your hands. Press together to form a moist dough. If it is really sticky add more flour.

2) On a floured surface roll out the dough until it is around 3–4mm thick – the same depth as the grains of suet.

3) Spread jam evenly over the surface, but not too thickly or it will ooze out and make a mess during cooking.

4) Now gently roll the flattened dough loosely like a Swiss roll.

5) Transfer it to a baking sheet covered in baking parchment. Cover the roll loosely with foil. I find that chilling it in the fridge for 30 minutes helps it fluff up when it cooks. Cook covered with foil for 20 minutes, then remove the foil for last 10 minutes of cooking. Serve hot.

SWEET 'N' SALT PEANUT BUTTER WHIP

Time: 15 minutes prep, as long as possible to chill, but can be eaten immediately if really necessary

365g Firm Silken Tofu pressed to give around 220g (see Skill Set, page 38)

1 tablespoon unsalted Smooth Peanut Butter

1 tablespoon Non-Dairy Margarine

1½ tablespoons dense vegan sweetener such as Rice Syrup

1 teaspoon Lemon Juice

Generous pinch of Sea Salt

4–6 drops of Almond Extract

Place everything into a food processor and blend until completely smooth. You will need to stop the processor and scrape the mixture of the sides of the bowl several times to ensure complete mixing.

Spoon into serving dishes and chill for around 6 hours for best results. Decorate with fruit such as bananas or raspberries or drizzle vegan chocolate over surface as shown.

SWEET 'N' SALT PEANUT BUTTER WHIP

TROPICAL YOGHURT TART

TROPICAL YOGHURT TART
with Ginger Oat Base

This tart is better eaten up within 48 hours, because the water from the soya yoghurt will slowly separate and soak into the base, making it very soft. The yoghurt needs straining for 12 hours, but the rest of the prep is quick and only needs chilling.

Serves 12 easily

Base

- 12 Ginger Snap biscuits
- 2 tablespoons Non-Dairy margarine
- 1 heaped tablespoon Golden Syrup (or Maple Syrup)
- ½ cup Rolled Porridge Oats

Tropical Yoghurt Centre

- 500ml Strained Natural Soya Yoghurt (starting with 1 litre of yoghurt which after straining gives halve the volume)
- 1½ tablespoons Almond Oil (or similar neutral tasting oil, although raw Coconut Oil works)
- ⅓ cup Sugar
- 1 teaspoon Lemon Juice
- 300ml fresh Tropical Juice Mix (50ml of this put aside)
- 2 tablespoons Agar Flakes / Powder

Topping

- 250ml Strawberry or Red Berry Juice and 1 tablespoon Agar

1) In a small saucepan gently melt the margarine and when melted take off the heat and add the syrup. Stir and set aside.

2) Crush the ginger snap biscuits using a plastic bag and a rolling pin. I tend not to use a processor to do this as it just creates dust rather than a nice crumb.

3) Place the ginger biscuits and the oats into the saucepan with the melted margarine and syrup and mix together thoroughly.

4) Line the base of a 7" spring sided tin with baking parchment.

5) Scoop out all of the ginger oat mixture into the tin and press down firmly with the back of a spoon or with a spatula. Chill in the fridge whilst you make the next part.

6) Into a clean saucepan, place the sugar, lemon juice, Tropical Juice (keep that 50 ml aside for later), and agar.

7) Heat gently until it is boiling, stirring continually. Once boiling turn the heat right down and simmer gently.

8) Stir as it simmers for 8 minutes for the agar to activate.

9) When this juice mix is ready pour it into a blender. Add to it the yoghurt, the extra amount of Tropical Juice and the almond oil and blend until smooth and creamy.

10) Pour all of the yoghurt mix into the tin with the chilled ginger oat base. Smooth and level, then chill in the fridge for an hour until set.

11) To make the gel topping simply place the agar and the strawberry juice in a pan and heat as before. Once at boiling point, simmer gently for 8 minutes. Spoon it onto the tart to avoid 'dimpling' and chill.

PLUM & ELDERFLOWER CRUMBLE

Time: 30 minutes prep and cook. Oven 210°C top shelf

8–10 large deep coloured Plums
2–3 tablespoons Elderflower Cordial
2 tablespoons Water
200g / 8 oz Plain Flour
30 – 50 g / 1–2 oz Rolled Porridge Oats

80–100g / 3–4 oz Non-Dairy Margarine
Generous pinch Salt
50g / 2 oz Demerara Sugar for topping
4–5 tablespoons Caster Sugar for fruit

1) Place ripe plums in a bowl and cover with boiling water. Leave for 5–10 minutes until the skins begin to split. Then replace the hot water with cold.

2) Peel the skins of the plums and cut chunks of flesh from the stone into an oven-proof baking dish that can hold 2 pints. The plums have already had a pre-cook when soaking so no need to stew them at all.

3) In a saucepan place the water, elderflower cordial and caster sugar and heat, stirring. Bring to the boil and then allow to simmer briskly, stirring occasionally until the colour deepens a little. This will form a thin syrup which you then pour over the plums.

4) Whilst the fruit and syrup cool and form a slight skin, pre-heat your oven making sure the shelf is on the highest rung.

5) Prepare the topping by placing all of the flour, oats, demerara sugar, salt and margarine into a mixing bowl and combining them with your fingers. Rub the ingredients between fingers and thumbs so that all becomes coated in the margarine and the mix looks like breadcrumbs.

6) Now here is my little trick. Squeeze handfuls of the mix together, then gently break apart again and do this over and over so that you have an uneven arrangement of various lumps and crumbs. This gives a better crunch than just having a fine breadcrumb texture.

7) Place the topping onto the surface of the plums carefully, handfuls at a time. Don't press it down in any way, just let it settle, levelling it to make sure there is an even amount all over.

8) Now the second tip is to bake it hot and quick. This browns the topping without causing too much of the syrup to seep into the crust and making it too soggy. 15 minutes is plenty of time to cook the whole thing perfectly. Serve hot with custard or cream.

MOIST CHOCOLATE SPONGE TRAY BAKE
with Jam & Toasted Coconut

This is a fail-safe chocolate cake that works well hot with custard or cold with the topping shown.

Time: 15 minutes prep, 20–25 minutes baking. Oven 170°C

175g / 7 oz Self Raising Flour
50g / 2 oz Raw Cacao Powder
3 teaspoons Baking Powder
85g / 3½ oz Non-Dairy Margarine
100g / 4 oz Caster Sugar
2 tablespoons thin Vegetable Oil

1 tablespoon honey substitute (i.e.; Agave Nectar)
1 teaspoon Vegg (if you don't have this then add another ½ teaspoon of Ener-G in place of it)
3 teaspoons Ener-G Egg Replacer
120ml Orange Juice
120ml cold Water

With any cake mix involving a powdered egg replacer and baking soda/powder, it is essential that once these items touch liquid they reach the oven within moments. They begin to work once they are mixed so preparation is key.

1) Prepare the tray bake tin (roughly 24cm square) by lining with parchment. If you smear the tin with margarine first the parchment will easily stick to the sides and you can push and fold the corners in neatly. Do this even if your tin is a non-stick type. The sponge will be fragile when it comes out of the oven and lifting it out using the parchment will stop it cracking apart, especially if you are serving it hot.

2) Prepare the egg replacer by measuring out the powder and placing it into a small blender or jug. Have the orange juice measured ready but DO NOT add to the powder yet.

3) Put your oven on making sure the shelf is in the middle.

4) Place the margarine, sugar, and oil into a mixing bowl and blend together. Then with a fork or a hand whisk, whisk together until it looks quite frothy. Add the Agave nectar and whisk that in.

5) Now sieve the flour, cacao powder and baking powder into the bowl, but don't mix it up just yet.

6) Add to the bowl the water, but again don't mix it.

MOIST CHOCOLATE SPONGE TRAY BAKE

7) Now add the orange juice to the egg replacer and whiz together to make it as frothy in 20 seconds as you can .

8) Add this liquid to the mixing bowl and now you can mix everything together very quickly, almost like beating it together. It will resemble a mousse full of big air bubbles as the egg replacer and baking powder start to work.

9) Now scrape it all into the tray, in one big dollop if you can and smooth it out quickly. This doesn't have to be perfect, just roughly level and into the corners. Now get it into the oven and bake for 25 minutes. It is cooked when a knife can be pushed into the cake and it comes out clean.

10) Allow the cake to cool in the tin for five minutes, then using the baking parchment lift it out and place on a cooling rack.

You can serve this straight away with custard or let it cool, smother in seedless raspberry jam and top it with toasted coconut.

Tip: Toast desiccated coconut by putting into a dry frying pan and gently heating, stirring all the time. But don't let it burn. Once it starts to go golden it catches very quickly. It is also very hot so don't touch it until you have allowed it to cool down.

COFFEE SPONGE CAKE WITH CHOCOLATE BUTTER CREAM

Time: 15 minutes prep, 30–40 minutes baking. Oven 150–160°C

150g Non-Dairy Margarine

150g Caster Sugar

300g Self Raising Flour sieved with 2 teaspoons Baking Powder

¼ teaspoon salt

4½ teaspoons Ener G Egg Replacer

6 tablespoons Orange Juice

3 teaspoons Coffee Extract

2 teaspoons granulated instant coffee in 1 teaspoon boiling water

½ tablespoon Vanilla Extract

Frosting:

1 tablespoon Raw Cacao Powder

2 tablespoons Margarine

Icing Sugar (as much as you want)

1 teaspoon Coffee Extract

Crushed toasted nuts to decorate

1) Prepare one 7–8" tin or two 6–7" tins with parchment. See the Skills Set section 'Lining Tins' (page 42) for help with this.

2) Checking the shelf is placed in the middle, pre-heat the oven.

3) In a mixing bowl place the margarine and the sugar and cream together with a wooden spoon or hand whisk.

4) Sieve in the flour and baking powder, add salt and all of the extracts and the coffee water. DO NOT STIR YET.

5) In a cup or in a small blender place the Ener-G egg replacer powder and the orange juice, and whisk together until foamy.

6) When the oven is ready, add the egg mix to the mixing bowl and quickly and thoroughly mix everything together. The mixture will immediately start forming air bubbles, so transfer it to the tin or tins, level roughly and get the tin/s into the oven. The quicker you do this the better.

7) Bake one tin for 40–45 minutes and two tins for 30 minutes. Check the sponge is cooked with a skewer or sharp slim knife blade, which if comes out clean means the sponge is cooked.

8) Allow cake to cool for five minutes before removing from the tin and to cool completely before placing the frosting on it.

9) The frosting is simply the mixing together of the ingredients until smooth.

10) For extra indulgence add toasted crushed nuts to the top.

Tip: As with all sponges, it is best to leave it a day before cutting as the sponge edges will soften.

DESSERT SAUCES

Choc Fudge Sauce

40g Plain or Milk Vegan Chocolate

75g Non-Dairy Margarine

3 tablespoons honey substitute

Simply place everything into a water bath (a bowl placed into a pan of warm water) and melt together. Turn up the heat until the mixture bubbles and stir continually for a couple of minutes. Remove from heat and drizzle over dessert.

For a nutty twang add some Roasted Cashew Butter or Peanut Butter.

Emily's Dream Topping

200g Firm Silken Tofu (pressed)

2 teaspoons Vanilla Essence

½ Lemon, juiced

125ml Non-Dairy Single Cream (or Rice Whipping Cream)

1 tablespoon honey substitute

Simply place everything into a processor and blend until smooth. You may wish to add a pinch of salt. Chill to thicken.

Thick Salted Date Syrup

1 cup pitted Medjool dates

1 cup water

¼ teaspoon coarse Salt

Optional addition of flavourings such as Rum, Coffee, Almond or Orange extracts

Place all ingredients into a processor and blitz until completely smooth.

ONE MEAL INTO MANY

Many of my recipes have come from the back end of another, sometimes one that hasn't worked well, or by an accidental combination of two flavours in the mouth. I remember eating a pecan and popping a little basil into my mouth just to see what it was like…that began a series of new patés, and when I accidentally added peel in with the mixed fruit in a stew, and it added a fresh zing to every other mouthful.

Being creative has nothing to do with being original. It is about being able to re-adjust an already existing 'thing' so that it has a different flavour, texture, or freshness. Vegan food is often like that anyway, because we try to take a dish we love as an omnivore and 'veganise' it.

So you make a Ratatouille, or a paté or a stew, and what do you do with it once the novelty has worn off? Or there are left-overs but not quite enough for a whole meal? Or you want to make a dish but haven't got two or three of the required ingredients? You improvise, and it is a skill that improves the more you try. It really isn't hard if you start with a few simple questions;

Can I eat it on toast?

Will it go on a baked potato?

Will it make a base for a soup or stew?

Can I whiz it up and make a dip?

Would it be good inside a pitta or a wrap?

Would it work as a pasta sauce?

What would it taste like fried?

You see what I mean? Every dish has a myriad of related dishes that it just takes a little hop of imagination to find. Not a leap, just a hop.

One of my favourite lunches is left-over veg in the fridge, fried. So a big mushroom, a couple of tomatoes, some mashed potato, baked beans, and some brown sauce! Not all mushed up together but kept separate and served just like a normal fry-up. Mmm.

Never throw out anything until you have exhausted all possibilities – or it has gone off!

One of the most annoying things is not having a vital ingredient for a recipe. I often give ideas about this in the recipe itself, alternatives and so on. But it would be great if you could just do this yourself. If you are making a journey of growth in the world of cookery, and like me you may feel ready to spread your own creative wings and get messy. I mean MESSY! That's when I make the best things when the kitchen looks like hell. With flour sifted all over it – and something sticky on the fridge door.

I am hoping you have a pretty good selection of spice, herb and condiments by the end of this book. This is your arsenal to turn a plain, innocent tomato or cauliflower into a sultry sauce or a seductive stew (yep, they can be seductive – they win men's hearts), or the sharp blackcurrant into a sweet whisper of luxury. Yes okay, a bit over the top, but you need to think a bit like this to delve into the food. It isn't just a few ingredients. It is chemistry for the senses.

I like to think of two new ingredients – by new I mean a combination I haven't tried before. Let's say apple and fig. Then I think about savoury and sweet alternatives. So a sponge, a tart with a glaze, a paté, maybe even a curry. Perhaps a sweet and sour salad, or a paste for going inside a flatbread.

Start simply, and use a foundation you know works. If I make a new paté, I still use basic things like a slice of bread, plus chestnuts/nuts, plus dried tomatoes, because I know these give bulk, richness and texture. But I could add anything to it to create something new. I remember when I decided I was going to add apple and prunes to a paté. It made a rich dark but rather wet paté, so I decided to try baking it – it was amazing and became the Pecan & Red Wine Paté.

A good way to start creating your own things is to make something you know and add a new topping or filling. So create a frangipane with some new fruit on top and a glaze, or maybe Ratatouille with a new vegetable added or a spice. I do this all of the time, and find that every so often something magical happens and a new idea turns into a fresh new recipe. Nothing that original I don't suppose, since original doesn't really exist, but certainly fresh to me and my family. And that is what really matters to us, isn't it?

Me with one of our current rescue dogs, Fred

How did *Rooted* happen?

I like to share. And show off a bit too, I suppose: I think we all have a level of vanity if we are honest. For me it is the need to have my creativity shown and then enjoyed by others. Art and music have always been my platforms. Now it is my food and my writing.

Since I couldn't find the recipe book I wanted (and didn't really want to follow one anyway – yep, I am that contrary), I decided to make my own recipes up, and share those. To do this I followed the example of many, and started a Facebook page called *From Plant to Plate – Food without Fear* (which is now called **Fearless Vegan Food Blog**). I still keep it up-to-date today, so if you frequent Facebook, do come and join the page and enjoy further tips, recipes and shares. There is a sister page that gives out free recipes called **Fearless Vegan Recipes**. (I also have a Facebook page for all of my writing both non-fiction and fiction called Author Sarah Jay/number1crimewriter.)

Initially I thought my recipe attempts were pretty bad, but I would photograph them as nicely as I could and post them, explaining my difficulties and hoping that someone would advise where I was going wrong. Strangely, so I thought, no one seemed to. Instead, the page picked up interest through people's perception of my food's traditional looking plating and use of everyday ingredients, most of which was available from supermarket shelves.

I began to quickly realise that a lot of self-help vegans were struggling and living on very little that was varied or interesting and they saw even my 'failures' in the kitchen as new alternatives to their usual bean burgers or tofu kebabs. I had no idea so many vegans were badly informed about cooking. In many cases it was like the blind leading the blind, with the same bean burgers and lentil burgers being passed around in perpetuation! The first comment I got about my Quinoa, Carrot, Cajun & Ginger Pattie recipe was 'Oh thank you – I am so sick of my bean and chickpea burgers!'

The nice thing about a lot of vegans is that they support a fellow vegan's efforts – all are worthy. I soon began to get requests for recipes and I began to give a few out. In just three weeks my personal page clocked up 700 likes, and in just three months, it had over 1700 likes. In another three months, 2000 likes. In another three, 3100 likes. I joined lots of groups who were interested in vegan and earth friendly foods, and I began to really get the feeling that I had hit on something a little different. I was one of the few who wanted to eat things other than tofu, kale and chickpeas, and liked my gravy, pies and dumplings. Lots of vegans did **not** want to pursue optimum super-health or go without the food that comforted them and made them feel at home.

Around the same time my partner bought a new camera which really revolutionised the way I took the photographs. I became taken with the whole food photography thing and realised how powerful a good photograph can be. With a bit of arty direction and some new second-hand dishes and tablecloths, I was able to take homely but clear images of food. Having said this, I have difficulty with light, and still find the best spot for photographs is the kitchen draining board. It isn't very glamorous but it works. The pictures did look better and the response proved it to be the case. The comments began to reflect some ideas I was having. 'You know you should turn this into a book, your site is so beautiful,' one lady wrote.

I had been looking for a focus for my life, having tried various jobs and not feeling I really fitted in any of them. I am quite an unusual person, impulsive, creative, self-reliant and bipolar, so I have challenges to face each time I find myself in a full-time job working within other people's set expectations. I work much better as a self-managed person doing something I have a passion about. For a long time teaching music from home was what I did, but only part-time. I have been very fortunate to always have the security of a partner who supports my activities and projects, even though I have tried virtually every sort of job going.

To seriously write (and finish) a fully formed book of any kind, you need a focus, a passion. I know because I have tried before; a short novel, some poetry, a play, nothing that really worked. But this was different. A book that I wish I could have read when I began to live as a vegan. Although there are plenty of free recipes online, the immediacy and collection of recipes in book or eBook form is always useful and still very much favoured by a lot of home cooks. And mine would also be the reader's companion, with advice and encouragement and pages where they could write their own notes, feelings and concerns and where they could turn to be reminded that all their failings, like mine, are part of the transition, the journey. It is also where you could find some solace when faced with the teasing and questioning of those around you, how to deal with those who just 'don't get it' like you do.

Finally, my partner and I discussed the option of me stopping work as a piano teacher, and concentrating on cooking and writing. I think he could see my enthusiasm and the keen response my Facebook page was getting. And so, that is what I did. I thanked my good man that I was able to do this, and was not forced to work for pay at that time. He has been my rock and partnered me as a vegan from day one, along with both my children.

I don't think I believed I could actually do it at first. The belief grew as the number of recipes grew. Once I started, taking the photos, writing up the recipes and loading them onto my pc, I got into a flow, and decided to try and add something new every day. That waned pretty soon (I seem to remember that rate of production lasting around four days). I did manage at least one or two new recipes a week, which includes the magnificent failures as well as the successes.

I truly believe that vegan food shouldn't be food that you have to get used to over time, but food that is instantly liked because it tastes good, has lovely textures and looks familiar as well as alluring.

That isn't to say I never had days where I just wished I could order a take-away or fish and chips. I do get very tired some days and find it hard to motivate myself, so those days were tough. But in being tough I learnt how to get through and I have shared that knowledge with you in this book. Life gets in the way of many of the things we set out to do, and that is very true in family life, so I hoped to keep that in mind when writing and inventing meals.

I have new ideas all of the time and my passion has not wavered, even though cooking is not my favourite activity, and I constantly resist looking up how to achieve certain cooking goals. Becoming vegan has forced me to become productive and creative in the kitchen and now it is the means to a new and wonderful life. So don't feel you have to be a great cook or even like cooking that much to enjoy this journey. Nor do you really need to stick to recipes – I certainly didn't and still don't, not even to my own. In fact writing down everything I did so that I could relate it to others has been the hardest part of this whole venture.

I realise that many people do not have the time to spend in the kitchen as I do, or scouring shops or online suppliers for foodstuffs, so I hope this book provides you with short-cuts. But don't limit yourself. Once you get started, I am sure you will spread your own culinary wings and not need a book like this forever. That is my goal for you as the author.

Some of the hardest aspects about being vegan are linked to living amongst so many non-vegans, most of whom are ignorant of what veganism really is or what vegan food encompasses. All of society will suddenly seem to challenge you at every turn. Be prepared. You will experience a frustration like no other, and I do give you some advice from my own experience on how to deal with this. Also on other things such as shopping, eating out and getting enough nutrition. I am not a nutritionist, so this book does not aim to give you a daily menu or tell you what to eat. That is for you to discover. Research is important, and I encourage you to do it for your own lifestyle and body type, not because you will be eating a vegan diet, but because it is sensible for everyone to do so.

Certainly if you have any medical issues, do have a chat with a doctor before you embark on a vegan diet. I would advise against cutting out caffeine, sugar and fat at the same time, if this is also one of your goals. This shocks the body and depresses you mentally and physically. One step at a time.

So for whatever reason you are reading this, I hope it brings you interest, some laughs and some motivation to follow a vegetarian or vegan life, at least in as far as eating goes. This is not a book about the complete vegan lifestyle. Nor is it a campaign book. I am not an activist. I am gentle, kind and patient. I believe that change has to come from within an individual and it needs to be motivated by that person's will. And will, cannot be forced.

Do enjoy this time in your life, and I hope this book is part of that enjoyment.

My Own Reasons for Being a Vegan

Remember, this book is not trying to convert you. But I am sure you have asked yourself already 'Why did she?' or 'What drove her?' or something similar. So I shall put it simply here. You may or may not share my motivation.

I love animals. That's it, really. I love them and I realised I was living a hypocrite's life if I said I loved them and at the same time I ate them. I also knew I would not eat them if I had to slaughter them, or if I saw the state many of them are raised in, and the abuse that is commonplace from the moment they are born to the point of slaughter. And that was the basic feeling I had, all my life. Except I didn't do anything about it until I was 45 years old. Why, is the substance of another book entirely – and a very interesting one. It is the one part of this journey that fills me with shame, that I left it so long. That shame is part of the reason for this book, trying to put something wrong, right, by helping others to see the truth behind the gloss of what is industrialised farming and slaughter.

I was once an omnivore. Then I began to think for myself, and question assumptions and ignorance, not just about the ethical treatment of animals, but about our environment, population, food resources and world malnutrition. Veganism is a way for many issues in the world to be controlled and even reversed. There is much information about these issues out there if you want to find it.

Veganism is like wiping a slate clean and then enjoying making fresh marks upon it in a new set of colours.

And here we are only really touching on food. The lifestyle itself encompasses so much more. It is life based upon compassion, tolerance and moderation.

I know I cannot stop the suffering of animals on my own, just as I cannot stop human suffering by giving a meal to a homeless person. But doing nothing feels wrong. Standing up and doing something is a start, a hope that more will follow my example. The ocean is, after all, only a conglomeration of water droplets. Perhaps becoming vegan really is the one biggest positive environmental change that an individual can make. It is about more than not eating meat or wearing fur, it really does affect every aspect of human existence on the planet, in turn benefiting the Earth's fauna and flora.

I am proud that I miss the taste of certain foods that I choose not to eat, because I have faced up to what it means to eat them. That is crucial. The choice.

Being vegan does not mean you can no longer have certain foods. It means you choose not to eat them, not to partake.

That can take real will power on days of extreme tiredness, or depression, on days when you go out with others and the pressure is on you to 'follow' social trend. I am proud. That makes me strong.

Becoming vegan is a mini battle because our world is so pro-animal exploitation in everything, everywhere, and as non-vegans we are unaware just how vast, how deep the extent is. Becoming vegan requires you to open your eyes, probably for the first time, to things society has conditioned you to be blind to. There is a reason slaughter houses do not have glass walls, that there are not school trips to factory farms. Sometimes you wish you had never asked to see the truth, for it can be a burden, but animals only have us to speak out for them. Slowly, we are listening.

For me, civilisation means compassion and respect. It doesn't mean humans come first.

First Errors

I am a clearer-outer by nature, not a hoarder. I like nothing better than to have a good sort-out, even when it isn't my stuff that I am throwing out, much to the chagrin of my partner and my children. I re-cycle a lot, and try not to buy what I don't need. I still end up with a lot of 'stuff'. I really do not know where it comes from (and I think many of you recognise yourselves here)!

So when I decided one evening that the time had come for me to make the change from omnivore to vegan (and I still don't know why it was that particular evening), I went into the kitchen and emptied all my cupboards and fridge, removing everything that was non-vegan and getting shot of it. Yes, I threw it out. This was very wasteful of me and I wouldn't advise anyone do this. Give the food away or use it up.

I told my partner that I would be cooking differently from now on and he nodded; his usual calm response to most things. He didn't even query the activity in the kitchen until he realised the bourbon biscuits and the Cadbury's Fruit & Nut had disappeared.

There seemed to be things that vegans must have in their larders (I found this out after a whole evening of research – yes, a whole evening), things like Tofu, pulses, lentils, agave, inactive yeast, tahini, flax and hemp and lots of bohemian-sounding items that had me foxed but intrigued. I was too busy purging and ordering to think about what I was going to be eating or what I would do with these new ingredients. I ordered still more: chickpeas, spices, egg replacer and nuts. And all this without even having taken stock of what my supermarket had in way of vegan supplies. I think I assumed there wouldn't be very much, which was a misguided assumption on my part. It was also a sign that I hadn't really a clue what vegan food was, or could be.

Even though I had bought a couple of vegan cookbooks a few weeks previously, having a feeling in my gut that change was imminent, I had simply (though very proudly) placed them between biscuit and pasta jars on the worktop, and left them there. I didn't read them! Not until I had already ordered 6 boxes of Ener-G Egg Replacer, and several kilos of raw chickpeas. I didn't even know what cooked ones tasted like! And now I know I don't actually like them. That is the point I am making here. I didn't do enough reading or thinking first.

My excitement when the food parcels arrived, the boxes cut open and packets and tins carefully eased out with trembling fingers, quickly became a throat-tightening fear as

I peered into my heaving cupboards now packed snuggly with foreign foods like gifts waiting to be wrapped. I mean, what was Agave Nectar!! Nutritional Yeast?? What was Tahini used for? Dipped in a finger and, oh God, it tasted revolting!

I had not started my journey well. My family were hovering in the doorway awaiting the first vegan feast. I wanted to run out of the back door.

I made a big cup of tea. I took out one of the pristine vegan cook books, sat down and began to look at the contents page – it had no pictures.

I have always been a keen cook, a lover of good food, if a little simple. I come from a family of non-cooks, although my Nan (my Mother's Mum) loved baking and did a mean Christmas Dinner. Going to her house for Sunday tea was a regular thing. Out would come Victoria Sponge as deep as your forearm, strawberry jam oozing out of its sides, Curd Tarts with tiny currants in them that tasted salty and sweet all at once, and the Blackcurrant Pie that only happened when the fruit was in season. Cutting into the crisp pastry would release the purple-black syrup that tasted sour to my young taste-buds, but came with the black jewels I would grow to adore. But other than making sweet delights, my Nan didn't like cooking at all. Nor did my other Nan whose menu was the same every week, and she cooked only three sweet things; Apple Pie, Coconut Cake and Bread Pudding. But those three things were the best of their kind anywhere. Funny how my childhood food memories are of the sweet things I ate. Apart from dumplings, I don't really remember savoury foods.

No one really explored outside the basic English working man's type of grub in our family, the lamb and pork chops, mashed potatoes and a piece of fish on a Friday. As a child and teenager I didn't know what a lasagne or a moussaka were, and spaghetti came in a tin that went on toast. Meals were very simple and most were cooked from scratch, with things like tinned peaches and evaporated milk or prunes and custard for pudding, which at least made them reasonably healthy.

Where I got my love of experimenting I don't know, probably from my natural creative energy that flows into everything I do. But it really blossomed when I had children. I wanted to cook everything from scratch so I knew what went in to my children's mouths. I even made my own baby food – carrot, broccoli and rice pressed through a sieve, poached pears and squashed banana with milk.

What I am saying is, I didn't have a broad cooking knowledge to start with, to be able to shift to a new way of cooking all on my own. I didn't have anyone to ask who could show me a few things, lend me an old family vegan recipe. But what the evidence in this book will prove is that if I can radically change what and how I cook, so can you. You don't need special skills. And I hope that some of my recipes will get handed around and eventually down to new generations.

Before you read on, it would be fun to just see what you think of as vegan food. You may of course be well informed already, and this may be a pointless exercise, but if you are new to this and up to now haven't thought much beyond looking at one or two books in a bookshop, then just use this page to note down as many foods as you can that vegans eat. Also try to say what nutritional group they belong to, so for meat you would have put protein and maybe fats. If you do this now, and then again in a few months, you may surprise yourself.

Vegan foodstuff	Nutritional group

Make a List

If you are now thinking about your own kitchen stores, it is a good time to take a look. You will surprised by how much is actually vegan in your kitchen, only you never thought of it that way before. Baked beans, Marmite, crumpets, a lot of cereals, lentils, non-egg pasta, rice, fruit and veg, nuts, dried fruit, peanut butter, golden syrup, many ketchups, jam, chips, tea, coffee, fruit juice, noodles and so on. The things that are not vegan such as dairy and eggs, don't throw them out. Use them up or give them to a friend. Waste is a terrible thing.

Just remember that there is already so much potential in what you already have. With a few simple and recognisable additions you can actually come up with some really good vegan food.

This may seem a bit obvious, but how do you know what is vegan and what is not? Well, lots of foods are now labelled as 'vegan', though a single green V does not denote this. That could just mean vegetarian. If there is no vegan label, look at the ingredients and check for the obvious – dried dairy or egg products, whey or things like 'natural protein derivative' which sounds very suspect to me. Right now you are concerned about the obvious. Don't worry too much about the fine detail. You can sort that out as you learn more, and become a discerning consumer. Take a look at the section 'Integrity of Ingredients' (page 241) for a little more advice on this.

I would also advise you phase-in your vegan eating. We tended to continue eating fish and eggs until I had enough meals I could rustle up that were vegan. It took about six months. Dairy was easy to replace with non-dairy as there are so many alternatives in supermarkets now. You may have to try a few different milks to find the one you prefer. If you have eaten omnivorously for 40+ years, what difference do a few more months make as you transition? – as long as you reach the goal of becoming fully vegan eventually. That is the focus.

To help you phase in your vegan cookery, I have added a key to the list of recipes to show those that are quick, easy and raw. Choosing these first will give you a foundation from which you can move forward with your own idea. If you haven't done so already, I would suggest you take a look through the recipe list and choose a few that are easy to start with, noting down any ingredients you will need to get. There really aren't any original ideas anymore, just re-jiggled ones, so try not to feel over-awed by overly complicated recipe books and programs. Try to keep to the ones you feel comfortable with and grow in confidence with them.

It would be a good idea to write down the foods you have that are vegan here, so that you can refer to it as you look at the recipes. Things like mixed dried fruit, which you have probably only ever used in fruit cake, is used in several of my savoury dishes for instance. The interesting question is, how much of what is vegan in your kitchen, did you actually write down on the first list of vegan food and its nutritional group? I suspect you might have missed out some obvious things!

Foods you have that are vegan:

Foraging in the Aisles

This is a proud moment, a red carpet moment! Of course the supermarket and its shoppers will not be aware that you are entering through its doors as a new vegan, but feel good about it. They soon will. You are about to experience a sense of pious self-importance over your fellow shoppers, particularly at the checkout when all of your beautiful, fresh, colourful array of produce is laid out.

Ingredients that I use every week and are used throughout this book are listed here in case you like to have some guidance. More obvious items that are probably already in your cupboards, such as plain flour, jam and fruit, have not been listed. There are also many helpful online lists for the vegan pantry. Such lists are quite personal really, so try not to stick too rigidly to them. As I have already mentioned, choose a few recipes and sort which ingredients you will need for them. Adding on to your already existing pantry is the best way forward. Buy small amounts of new things until you know you like them. Then think about ordering bulkier quantities of expensive things, like nuts and seeds, online.

- 2 Packs of **Firm Silken Tofu**
- **Rolled Porridge Oats**
- **Non-dairy products from chiller**: low salt margarine (soya or sunflower or olive based), soya or nut milk (use light flavoured) soya or nut cream, plain and fruit yoghurt
- Ready cooked **Sweet Chestnuts**
- **Mix of Seeds**
- **Various Mushrooms**
- **Mixed Dried Fruit**
- **Unsweetened Desiccated Coconut**
- **Nuts**: unsalted peanuts, cashews, pecans, hazelnuts
- **Soft Brown Sugar & Icing Sugar (NOT Royal)**
- Bag of fresh **Lemons/Limes**
- **Cooking Apples** (used in savoury & sweet dishes)
- **Fresh Garlic**

- Fresh **Ginger** (small piece)
- Tube of **Tomato Puree** and Pack of **Passata** (sieved tomatoes)
- **Sun Dried Tomatoes** both in and out of oil
- **Light and Dark Soya Sauce**
- **Marmite** (even if you hate the stuff, it is used as a seasoning, and can't be tasted as Marmite)
- Packet of **Red Lentils**
- **Wholewheat Noodles**
- Small packet of **Polenta** (ground maize, sweetcorn)
- Various sorts of **Rice (brown, red and Basmati)**
- Thickeners & Gelling Agents: **Arrowroot** powder (in bakery section), **Corn flour**, some **Agar Flakes**.
- Smooth unsalted **Peanut Butter / Cashew Butter**
- **Ground Almonds**
- White and Malted / Various **Bread Flours**
- Tin of **Dried Active Yeast**
- **Lyle's Golden Syrup**
- **Egg substitute** – you will probably have to order this. Ener-G Egg Replacer (and occasionally Vegg) are the two I use. You may be lucky and your shop may have one – best to ask!
- Non-Dairy **Dark Chocolate** (look in your supermarket's 'Free From' aisle)
- **Chocolate Hazelnut Spread** (a must in our house – in the 'Free From' aisle)
- **Raw Cacao Powder** – not 'cocoa'; you will probably have to order this online or get from a health food shop.
- **Honey Substitute** (I use Sweet Freedom and Agave Nectar, Maple Syrup and Golden Syrup)
- Herbs and Spices; A good **Salt** (Rock or Sea used for grinding – not table salt), **Garlic Salt**, Dried **Mixed Herbs**, Dried **Tarragon**, Dried **Basil**, Dried **Bay Leaves**,
- **Curry Powder** (mild & medium), **Garam Masala, Ground Cumin, Balti Mix, Ground Coriander, Fennel Seeds & Nigella Seeds** (if you are going to make Naan

flavoured bread), **Chillies** in whatever form you want as long as you have some dried powdered or ground chilli too.(I dislike heat so I use it sparingly but will indicate in recipes when you can let rip with it if you desire).

- **Fresh Herbs**; Try treating yourself to a small sample of any new or known herb in its fresh state – quite different from dried and lovely in salads and sprinkled on new potatoes, curries and in dips. I usually have at least **Basil, Rosemary, Chives** and **Flat Leaf Parsley**.

- **Natural Extracts**: Almond, Vanilla, Lemon, Coffee

- **Rum Flavouring**

- **Fruit cordials and Elderflower Cordial**

It is a good idea to go shopping on a quieter day, when you yourself are not rushed off your feet, and you have the urge to go foraging. By this I mean really looking down every aisle in your preferred supermarket and checking out what they offer vegans. Take a notepad with you. You will find a lot of choice in the 'Free-From' or non-dairy, non-gluten aisle, the international foods aisle, herbs, spices, oils and vinegar aisle and others besides. Look at their choice of tinned and fresh pulses (lentils, chickpeas and beans), and things like sun-dried tomatoes, ready-cooked quinoa, cooked sweet chestnuts (usually near the sage and onion stuffing mix) and Tofu. There should be chilled nut and soya milks with the dairy milk, non-dairy yoghurt, cream and margarine/spread with the dairy. You may even be lucky and find a vegan cream cheese. Some of these are quite good. Please take note that *lactose-free does not mean dairy free.*

I have found that lots of everyday items, not normally associated with vegan ingredients, are vegan. I like my supermarket's own brand of mini wheats, whole wheat noodles, some of the popular brands of bread, pitta bread, cooking wine and ginger nuts for instance. Of course, anything from the vegetable and fruit aisle will be good, and nuts, seeds and flours too. Take care though. Things like the salad dressings you can find with the salad items contain dairy and or egg, as do many Quorn products. Vegetarian is not vegan.

It will take a few trips to get to know what your shop has, and it may vary from week to week. But know this. The change in your shopping habits will be noted by the supermarket. You will be making your mark, a small one but a significant one. With the choices you make and the pattern of spending you exhibit from now on, you send a message to the supermarket – there is a need for them to listen and cater more for the ever growing numbers of vegetarians and vegans. You are now a part of that change.

It is also time to be vigilant about other shops and independent retailers who might cater for your dietary needs. Fresh and local produce is always best, and local farms often sell direct to the public through a farm shop. Things like country fairs and festivals are good places to spend an afternoon hunting down pickles and jams, fruit and veg that might be of rare variety or made and grown in traditional ways. Think differently about food – it is an adventure.

**Foods you need to get /
foods you would like to try**

Home with the Groceries

So you bring home the bags full from your foraging trip, and your cupboards and fridge are now bursting with healthy produce. What to do next? Well, don't do what I did and panic. Make a cup of tea, as I did that first day, and then maybe another one, leaf through the recipe section again, and start simple and small. Look at the recipe list and look for the cherry logo, meaning **Easy**. Most are in this category so look for something familiar or with few ingredients. If you are a bit of a novice in the kitchen then these recipes will be best to start with.

Build from a base that is simple and easy, and keep to that level as long as you feel like it. Quick pasta, rice, stir-fry and salads with flat bread is always a good start, along with a nut paté and one of the oatie selection as these serve well as in-between-meal energy snacks. A curry or stew is also easy as long as you prepare ingredients as instructed.

Don't be afraid of making mistakes. Remember, you can still supplement your diet with some dairy and maybe eggs, or maybe a little fish. It will take a while for your body and taste buds to get accustomed, and for your cooking skills to adjust. We did this – and I don't care what the Alpha Vegans of this world say. It is better to make the transition your way than no way at all.

Please do not be put off by other people mocking your efforts. Those ignorant comments like 'Oh so you still eat eggs do you, so you aren't actually a vegan yet then' or 'For God's sake, you can't be 90% vegan! It's 100% or you are NOT a vegan'. Or the familiar, 'Oh why did you have to go and be a vegan? Now I don't know what to cook you when you visit – couldn't you just have some ham or something? Or maybe bring your own food? Yes that's it, bring your own.'

For the first few weeks we ate a lot of fruit salad with soya yoghurt and honey (not strictly vegan, and I no longer eat honey, I use fruit or tree syrups), baked beans on toast with lashings of brown sauce (using my own bread which was really filling and wholesome), milkshakes using almond or oat milk, fruit and seeds (now they call them smoothies), and a lot of my own energy bars which I call 'oaties'. Handfuls of pecan nuts, soya, fruit, yoghurt and salad also featured a lot and I learnt how to make my own stir fry sauces by looking at the ingredients on ready-made packets I liked. It is surprising how little we need, really.

We are so used to eating a different meal every day. Of wasting left-overs. It helps a lot if you let go of what you thought of as a meal for a while. It really helps. Think simple, fresh and let your old ideas of what goes with what go out of the window. You will soon know how to use left-overs and waste very little food.

Eating less than you used to will probably be a good thing, as long as you eat enough nutrition and calories. Now to be frank, I still don't know (or care) how many calories an average woman in her forties (who does no exercise and is only 5'2" tall) should be having every day, or how many microgrammes of calcium, iron, Vitamin B and all of that I am supposed to be having. I never have known and I never will. I know that we are paranoid about diet, which when you think that British people were on the whole, far healthier when rationing, seems ridiculous. I do think it is a money-spinner for some, wanting us to worry constantly about what we put into our bodies. If I feel tired I will eat purposefully more green leafy veg and fruit, and if I feel low I will make sure I am consuming plenty of oils and getting fresh air. But I will not give up my sweet tooth, although as a vegan I now know about sugar alternatives that are healthier and as for puddings and desserts, the vegetable alternatives for dairy are amazingly helpful when keeping an eye on the waistline, and the purse.

Having said this, it is always good to get used to trying healthier options and I am approaching this myself more and more. A future book will definitely include healthier options and more wholefoods.

Integrity of Ingredients

Whilst I would recommend you don't become anxious about everything you buy at this early stage, it is worth mentioning a few ingredients here to help you steer clear of obvious vegan no-goes. It will go towards what will probably become your ever increasing knowledge and curiosity about what you are eating, where it comes from, what processes have been used and just how vegan the product is.

You may well be ahead of me here. But before I was vegan, I had little idea about basic processes used in creating foodstuffs. I had no idea that isinglass was the swim bladder of a sturgeon and was used in brewing for instance. Nor did I know bones are used in a process to whiten sugar – now banned in the EU, I am assured by a trusted source, although still widely used in the US.

I thought intensive farming of pigs and cows was limited to the US, but that is not so. Sadly the pressure of increasing population means intensive farming is becoming widespread and more intensive. Many animals only see the sky on the way to slaughter. Roaming in pasture is really not possible anymore, and even dairy cows are becoming tethered to sheds. There are many that get exported alive from the UK to other countries where animal rights do not exist on any level at all.

I have always thought that food labelling can be misleading. I never feel quite ready to believe a vegan label unless I check it out with the food producer on their official website. Many food manufacturers are only too glad to answer a query by email about their products. A case in point is when I contacted both Tate & Lyle and De Kuyper by email with regards using their products in this book. Both manufacturers readily answered about the ingredients and processes used.

Supermarkets and large food manufacturers such as Heinz provide pdf lists of the vegan products they store or manufacture, usually available by simply searching 'vegan food list' for that brand or store. These are usually lengthy and tedious to look through, and personally I prefer spending time walking around a shop and looking directly at products I would like to use and seeing if there is a vegan alternative. Unfortunately, there never seems to be anyone who works at a supermarket that knows anything about vegan products beyond their location in the shop.

A couple of good Facebook groups who will answer queries about how vegan a product is are Vegan (Supermarket Finds) UK and 100% Vegan Products. PETA is also another good way, as is asking The Vegan Society. There are literally hundreds if not thousands of websites dedicated to educating us about vegan issues. Ignorance is no longer a valid excuse for the continuation of animal exploitation. I have included some useful sites I have used in the Useful References section (page 266).

It might be an idea to start a little notebook of foods to avoid, or additives etc. that are animal derivatives disguised as something else. Such things as E120 which is actually carmine or cochineal, a red food colouring made from a beetle *Dactylopius coccus*; 'Lactose free' which does not mean dairy-free; meat alternatives like Quorn that contain milk and egg derivatives; and Vitamin D which when added as 'fortified' can mean derived from animal sources (but not in all cases).

One interesting fact learnt recently is that glycerine, which I had assumed came only from animals, can also be obtained from plants. So if this ingredient is in a food such as icing, or a cosmetic like a shampoo, check to see if they say 'safe for vegetarians' or similar, or check online. Remember anything with the Leaping Bunny mark means it is cruelty-free.

The substance gelatine, which can get confused for glycerine, is unfortunately only obtained from bones so is never vegan. However there are many substitutes, including vegan gel in supermarkets.

This is an area that is actually a continual learning curve for all vegans, because products' ingredients change on a daily basis, as do supermarket label strategies and the use of the terms 'vegetarian' and 'vegan friendly'. At this stage in your transition, think of the bigger picture, rather than the fine detail. Think about cutting out the meats, fish, poultry, dairy, eggs and building confidence in what you believe and feel. The rest happens of its own accord over time. It is so easy to become bogged down in trying to check every single ingredient in every product that you eventually feel there is nothing but the fruit and veg aisle left to you. Believe me there are the very *very* well researched vegans out there who will jump down upon you with their own brand of wrath should you forgo to check the ingredients on those vegetarian muffins, but don't pay any heed. Those people are in every walk of life. Listen to what they have to say by all means, learn from it if it is indeed educational, but then walk on with a 'thank you kindly' bow of the head. Then continue with your own method and timetable of transition.

There are quite literally entire books dedicated to this topic alone and I have only briefly touched the surface. Regards labelling of ingredients in this book the Golden Syrup I use is Tate and Lyle's, and from their very email I was assured that it is indeed a vegan product – even though it says vegetarian on the tin! See what I mean about labelling. I was also concerned since I knew Tate was an American company that had bought out

Lyle's, and bone charring is still practised in some US states. I needed to be sure the syrup wasn't a product of those states.

Don't be fooled by vague, generic terms like 'Only Natural Ingredients', 'Green and Environmentally Friendly', 'Just Nature' or anything else – if it doesn't say categorically VEGAN anywhere on the packet, check before you buy. Many products still don't state they are suitable for vegans when they are, which is a real, frustrating, shame. See Useful References (page 266) for label and symbol clarification and sites for further information.

It is a great idea to keep track of ingredients that are not vegan but sounds harmless, or benign such as E120. As you learn you can add to the list.

Knowing & Sticking with your Onions

It isn't only the food issue you need to get to grips with as a vegan but also the attitudes of others. Believe it or not the first group of people with 'attitude' are themselves vegans.

They are what I call the 'Bully Alpha' Vegans, the ones who really hound people into either being 100% perfect from day one, or telling you not to bother if you can't commit to it. They like nothing more than being pious and arrogant and they do the cause of veganism no good in my opinion. I have myself been at the receiving end of some ridiculous bursts of what I can only call aggression from people who are supposed to be all about kindness, tolerance and compassion. One woman once posted to me on my Facebook page, after I mentioned I didn't like Quorn products, something along the lines, 'No vegan eats that rubbish because it has milk and egg in it. Any vegan knows that so I doubt you can be a vegan or at least you are a very new one. I doubt your recipes can be trusted based on your current understanding of veganism.' I recognised this lady's name from other posts she had made with similar acidic comments to other people. She must like living in her glass tower feeling better than everyone else. I would prefer not being associated with such a vegan. In fact, I would prefer not to be associated with any label at all. I eat food like everyone else, but I make certain choices about my food.

A better representation of veganism is portrayed by a group of vegans who are supportive, informative and realistic, what I like to call the 'Kindred' vegans. They appreciate that humans err occasionally and that temptation and pressure can cause will power to weaken. They also know that converting from omnivore to vegan is a process of transition, one that is unique to each person, driven by different motivations and that it takes a variable amount of time to get right. This group also includes friends and family who try to join in your desire to be vegan and willingly take part alongside you. This group are absolutely vital to your own journey and I suggest you join this group wherever and however you can.

The third group is probably the most difficult to deal with because they are the closest: friends and family and the rest of the public, who argue that you are wasting your time, don't know what you are doing and will probably die of protein deficiency, if the fad doesn't wear off before that. They are the ones who will constantly roll their eyes, ask leading questions that give them a chance to spout on about why they will always eat meat and make you feel you are only doing all of this for attention. You may well be accused of pushing your views onto them, even when you haven't actually opened your mouth. They are the ones who will frustrate you to tears if you are not careful. They may go as far as looking for the articles online that talk about plants having feelings, veganism at the root of the decimation of tropical rainforests, the whole gamut of misleading propaganda that is fuelled by the fear of those who make money from animal exploitation. They will also come out with ludicrous statements such as 'Well I couldn't give up meat because it just tastes too good' as if you never actually thought that once too, and 'Well if we didn't eat the cows what would we do with them instead?'

The lowest type of person you may encounter (and I use the word 'person' very loosely indeed) are the sadistic cowards, who like nothing better than to rub your face in as much slaughter gore as possible in the name of hunting, survival, sport or whatever they want to call it. I have had personal messages sent to me on social sites from male hunters of appalling and upsetting images, saying they are just for me. Now, I feel sorry for these obscenely sad people, for their need to bully and be so nasty, and their inability to feel the beauty and rights of other creatures, but I feel sorrier for the animals they kill. I don't ever give these people any of my time by replying to them, and I advise you do the same. Block them. I mention the type here simply to be honest about the vegan life, that it can attract some rather amoeboid types.

Alongside these four types of person is something buried deep within us. If you are like me, then your life to this point has probably been part of a culture that accepts there are meat, fish, poultry, dairy and egg aisles in the supermarket even though we watch with adoration natural history on TV, campaign against fox hunting, petition for the ban of the fur trade and vivisection, spend hundreds of thousands of pounds on vets, and even go as far as saving an injured wild animal from time to time. This socially conditioned hypocrisy goes deep into our psyche and physiology, fixing our senses to be alert to and stimulated by meat smells, the sight of meat, even the sound and thought of meat, but at the same time remaining disassociated from the industrialised suffering, abuse and slaughter of animals that become 'meat'. I include here everything that is omnivorous under the word 'meat'.

Not only are we brought up by our own families to accept this, to enjoy and partake and offer the same to our own children, we are never far from the bombardment of advertising, just in case we were ever doubtful how wonderful and necessary 'meat' was! From the selling of BBQ equipment to the Christmas Turkey, you are inundated daily by a powerful advertising machine that is designed to keep you buying what it wants you to buy. Cookery programmes, magazines, newspaper articles and posters, restaurants and by the road side-stalls, all push meat our way.

Do not underestimate the power of advertising over you. It is manipulative, clever and everywhere, and billions of pounds a year is spent worldwide to keep you doing what it wants you to do. As long as the industrialised meat, dairy and the rest are making money, money will be spent to influence what you think and do with your money. It is not easy to overlook this, especially if it is advertising the very thing you are missing the taste and texture of, like cheese for example. Or a thick, juicy steak. Plus those advertising invest money in research to find reasons why we shouldn't be going vegan, encouraging research into whether plants have feelings, or whether a plant-based diet would wreak environmental disaster. Vegans are often the butt of a joke about malnutrition, cult beliefs or crazy idealism. You need to be selective about what you read and what you believe, and who you take any notice of.

Temptation is your biggest enemy. Right now I am sitting with the patio doors wide open, as we happen to be having one of those unusually hot summer days, and I know it won't be long before the smell of fire-lighters and the stench of burning fat from last year's BBQ fest, will start to waft in. Garden after garden starts to send a smoke signal up, saying: 'Time for the ritual sausage and burger burning!' Luckily for me I was never a fan of the BBQ, but I know that for many it is a heavenly smell and for the male, a rite of passage to the caveman genes that lurk beneath the cultivated, civilised exterior. The chemical signals in your brain make you salivate, your stomach releases acid readying itself for some succulent delight. The smell may trigger memories of pleasant times spent with loved ones, maybe even a first date, on a beach holiday where you tasted your first grilled sardine fresh from the ocean. You are lost in thought.

But then a red flag springs up. You aren't allowed! You shouldn't be thinking about steak and lamb cutlets with juicy red wine sauce and salmon fillets dripping with butter… you are NOT ALLOWED NOW, YOU ARE VEGAN!

S T O P .

Stop right there.

Firstly, you are not forbidden by anyone NOT to eat a steak. That is crucial, as I mentioned before. **You are making a choice not to eat the steak.** Why? Well that is your own business, but for me it is because I know what it cost the cow, what the process is that gets that cow to the plate, and I am also becoming aware of the health benefits of not eating it. Your motivation might be different. You may have been told by a nutritionist or doctor that you must cut out meat from your diet. You may only be doing this to please your partner who has decided to become vegan. **Your brain is not fooled by any reason.** It wants that steak. It knows the satisfaction of eating it, its texture, its fulfilling flavour… Can just will-power be enough to overcome such temptation? I would say, in a lot of cases, no, if you continue to sit there in the path of the temptation. You need to boost your will-power by taking action, **setting yourself up to win.**

So, move away from the smell.

Go sniff a strawberry.

SERIOUSLY.

That is what I would do. Treat yourself to something yummy, or a bit naughty simply *because you are proud that you are resisting an urge that has been a part of you all your life*. It is like giving up smoking, or chocolate or drugs or drink. It doesn't matter how serious the reason for giving it up, it can be hard. Tuck into a piece of vegan chocolate, make a smoothie to die for, call someone for support, and go for a walk where there is space, sky and trees. And sniff a strawberry!

I know this all sounds a bit silly, but it is based on being in touch with nature, and this is actually crucial, and certainly the ability to empathise with nature and appreciate it grows with every vegan day that passes. I never thought I could be more pro-nature than I was, but I do feel much more sincere about it now. As often as you can, try to be close to animals. Look them in the eye, be aware of their warmth, their smell, their noises, and spend time watching them. There is so much there you have never seen before; you have been missing out on a privilege we humans have, to share another creature's space and quiet time, not just a dog's or a cat's but an animal that stands taller than you, that weighs the same as a small car and could trample you underfoot if it chose. Find out about the beauty and lives of the animals you have eaten. Go and find a farm where you can stroke down the soft face of a cow and look into its eyes. You will feel humbled when that cow looks right back at you with a gentleness you seldom see in human eyes. When a pig snuffles your hand with its sensitive snout and looks inquisitively at you with an intelligence to challenge many humans. These animals are not on earth for us. They are here with us. We don't need to kill them.

Those with the BBQs are still following the old way, the one they didn't choose but were conditioned to follow. You have chosen your way. You were once an omnivore. Then you began to think for yourself. That makes you strong.

Whatever has brought you to this change in your life, the reasons may not be obvious or logical to those around you. They may actually be genuinely worried about your health, even your sanity. There are so many nonsense facts going around about vegan diets, it isn't surprising that people think we fill ourselves up with a cocktail of supplements because the latest crank scientist claims humans aren't supposed to just eat plants. Most people are unaware that plants even possess protein, or that vegans eat a wider range of nutritious foodstuffs than most omnivores, and are better educated about human nutritional need. I can't believe the junk (and it actually gets affectionately called 'junk-food') people happily fill themselves up with whilst questioning those on a plant based diet (see the section 'The Protein & Cholesterol Confusion', page 260).

If you are in a situation where you are the cook, then go carefully and tolerate the family's possible reticence over your new 'venture'. They may think you will grow out of it. Introduce vegetarian foods and some vegan ones, but don't always announce that is what they are. Use your cooking to sway them, but in a gentle way. You can't force anyone to be a vegan. Try introducing them to your feelings through your food rather than through argument. Food brings people together.

Also involve the kids. Kids can be very awkward about food at the best of times. If you ban all their junk food and treats overnight and replace them with carrot sticks and nuts, they are not going to be amused – it doesn't matter how many lambs and calves are being considered, or whether Dad has been told he has to lose 60 lbs. Get the family involved in choosing new food items. The more involved anyone is in a project, the more likely it is they will want it to succeed. Get them leafing through the recipe pages and choosing things. Imagination will work wonders too. Try not to rely on salad and stir-fries. These become boring and lacklustre very quickly.

Remember too that I am still at an early stage myself. This book is only the beginning of my own journey, so see this as a hand to hold sometimes, a book to turn to for food ideas. It isn't a manual or a bible of any sort. As time goes on I will myself learn more, widen my culinary scope, and share it too. Keep up with my latest shenanigans on my Facebook page, Twitter and website. My details are in the Useful References section at the back of the book (page 266).

Veganism and Direct Action

Vegans are, by their nature, caring, compassionate and driven people. Many don't just get upset about the animals. So you may find that other vegans try to involve you in direct action or petitions about a hundred different things.

Some vegans develop to take things further, and become 'eco-warriors', and I know vegans who not only believe that veganism encompasses everything to do with life, not just refusing to eat sentient creatures or protesting against vivisection, but also believe in actively being part of educating others about world poverty, starvation, water shortage, deforestation, global warming, GM foods, pollution, refuse in the oceans, etc. It can seem to be a never-ending list of things that now, more than ever before, people feel compelled to do something about, and you may well become one of them.

It may become quite upsetting to see and learn of things you may not have been aware of before, and feel powerless to do anything about. I certainly have had days of complete numbness over what appears to be an overwhelming series of negative images, obscene lack of care from one human to another, a lack of care generally.

I know that going on marches, standing on street corners with a sandwich board and a megaphone or standing up in a restaurant and telling everyone about the processes of the food industry, is just not me at all. I am far too emotional to be useful in such scenarios, becoming tearful and aggressive at those that do not understand or won't listen. So I write, cook and share vegan food. That is my donation to helping put right all the difficult wrongs our times are living with. It may not seem heroic or action enough for some, but it is all I can do, as well as sign a few thousand petitions of course.

Being vegan doesn't mean you have to wear all of the badges of compassion. Do as much or as little as you want to, just try to keep a perspective. It doesn't have to all happen overnight, and it doesn't have to be you that does it all. That is asking too much of anyone.

Being vegan is the biggest gift we give to the planet, and to each other.

Making it Easier on You

Don't try to be a success in the kitchen every day!

Mistakes are part of life, cooking and decision making.

For goodness sake, have beans on toast and fruit salad and put your feet up.

It isn't wrong to have the same food or meal twice or thrice in a row.

Freeze extra portions for the days you are too tired or too busy to cook – or just can't be bothered. We all have those days.

Keep an interesting selection of fruit juices, fruit, nuts, dried and semi-dried fruit, seeds, vegan bars, yoghurt and other snack foods for pick-me-ups and quick lunches.

Do try to pick new fruits and veg to try.

Keep a special treat food which you adore, to use as congratulation to yourself for resisting temptation. It could be something as simple as a jar of Maraschino cherries or ready-made vegan custard. This could be something non-food related too.

Use up left-overs for a quick re-heated lunch or breakfast. Re-use left-overs to enrich or add to another dish.

When making vegetable stock, make as much as you can freeze and freeze it in small separate containers, serving size. This then provides you with a few weeks' worth of gravy or soup bases. The same can be said of soup or curry. These things freeze well.

Be patient with your family and friends – not everyone has reached the point you have, but it doesn't mean they won't one day.

Be especially patient with kids. They already have a lot to take in about the world and beating them over the head with your new found enthusiasm and truth about the meat industry might not have the desired effect. Try taking them to farms that allow you to integrate with the animals, or raise money for a sanctuary. Teach them animal ethics and love for nature. **And start getting them to help with the cooking.** They will thank you one day, as my son did when he went to university and had to cook for himself.

Please don't keep yourself on track as a vegan by pummelling yourself with animal cruelty images online. It will only depress you and make you angry. It is hard to motivate yourself and others into positive change when you use negative methods. Children are especially vulnerable to this. Remember that until now they have probably thought of farms as being like Old Macdonald's and hitting them with visual evidence of factory farms is not really terribly helpful. I have never believed in shock tactics. It is so much stronger when motivation is led by positive example, and being close to animals and forming relationships with animals will aid the change. Discussion about things is often better than using stark images. The latter simply labels vegans as people who try to ram their beliefs down others' throats.

If you want to get involved with animal activist activity I would keep to groups who do not use violence or damage property to make their statement. Positive change is made successfully using things as simple as banners and marches on a regular basis. It is persistence that wins. Recently a French restaurant in Soho, London, decided to stop selling foie gras paté because of a small group that assembled outside each lunchtime over several months, campaigning about the cruel way geese were farmed to produce this paté. The owner of the restaurant, who already had misgivings about it, was swayed by this demonstration, a demo that did not use violence or vandalism, but simple truth and compassion. A small but very significant example of what is happening everywhere.

Here is a chance to write your own motivational list of reminders – it matters!

I am not super-human – I will suffer temptation

I will make mistakes in the kitchen

Not everyone feels the way I do – be patient

I am strong for making this decision

It is fine to eat the same thing three days running

Eating Out

Eating out is something my partner and I don't do often enough (hint hint darling), but when we do, we enjoy it. That is because we go where we know there will be something good for us to eat.

Not such an easy thing to achieve if you are asked out on a date, to a fancy restaurant with the person of your dreams, only to find out they don't take your veganism seriously enough to have checked there is more than a salad and a bowl of chips waiting for you on the menu (and the chips might be cooked in beef fat or other).

It is times like these, along with many other examples like the 'Christmas Party' or 'work do' that can spell 's t r e s s' for the new vegan, because for some reason we feel guilty about being the odd one out, the nuisance, the attention-seeker that everyone else will have to cater for and perhaps in our English way, slightly embarrassed that we are 'different'. We may feel under pressure to go along with the majority and make do with whatever there might be on the menu for us. Probably yet another salad and baked potato. You may even try and reason with yourself; does it matter just this once? Well it is up to you, but if you would rather stick to your vegan plans, then maybe some of this might help.

One way to avoid feeling like this, is to do some research into local restaurants and then offer to do the booking yourself. It is easy for a meat eater to enjoy a meal in any restaurant, but it is not the same for a vegan. You may find your suggestion only meets with approval from the quiet friend who likes their comfy shoes and brings in a cake to the office each Friday, but at least you have shown yourself as willing to make the effort to make everyone else's meal experience stress-free. I don't know if you can hear that my tongue is wedged into the side of my mouth at this point. This option wouldn't work for everyone. I realise that some people are just not the organising type, or are too shy or don't have a position with enough political weight within the office hierarchy to even suggest such a thing. Yes, I have worked in office environments.

When planning to go out, or be taken out, phone the restaurant in advance. Peruse the menu online first if you can to see if there is a reasonable vegetarian choice (or even a vegan one – don't hold your breath), and ask if a vegetarian option could be tweaked to cater for a vegan. Now if their response is no, stay well clear of the place. As far as I am concerned a restaurant is only as good as its head chef, and that head chef is only as good as his imagination and endeavour to please his customers. But don't steer clear of a restaurant simply because they also serve meat and everything else that walks, crawls, slithers and swims. Doing this simply makes it easier for the restaurants to ignore us and continue unquestioned. If the restaurant staff suggest we find a vegan restaurant instead, then steer clear and tell everyone you know they are prejudiced! Facebook can be useful here.

Another way around the eating out awkwardness, is to actually take your friends, family and partner to a vegan restaurant. Most people have little idea what vegans eat beyond Tofu and green stuff, so surprise and delight those you love and show them that vegan can be extremely fun and delicious. Many of their preconceived ideas will be shattered the moment they smell the aromas and read the menu. But do make sure you try out the place yourself first or you may not be getting quite what you bargained for. Like any other restaurant, each is different.

I have to say that eating out is a better experience now because I no longer suffer from dry-meat disappointment, you know that moment when the food you ordered – that 'succulent steak with fries and seasonal vegetables cooked to perfection' arrives and it is actually dry, tough, and the vegetables are wet, soggy and sharing the same homogeneous taste. That doesn't happen to me anymore.

Just remember, don't sit there silently and try to please everyone else by eating whatever you can without complaint. Be proud. You have every right to eat well when a customer at a chef's pleasure.

You could of course, always practise your cooking skills and invite friends and family to a meal at yours. It can make all the difference to the level of support and appreciation – oh and respect, you get from there on in (and don't forget to use the attractive dishes and plates you have been collecting)!

Good places to eat vegetarian/vegan food

A Life-Long Purity

If I were to take a piece of cheddar cheese and eat it, my tongue and all of its taste buds, and my olfactory sensors would become coated and intoxicated with what used to be incorporated in my food every day: dense, congealed animal fat. My nose, where lies most of our sense of taste, would smell what it has been denied for over 24 months now. It would be revolted. I have tried it. I know. And I am not alone.

When you become vegan you may experience a revolution in the way your mouth, nose and brain process taste. There is a cleansed and much subtler set of flavours that seem to come into being once you stop coating your alimentary canal with animal fats. Even foods that you thought were familiar start to taste better. I found this was particularly true with fresh fruit and vegetables. I also began to enjoy flavours I hadn't liked much before, although I still had a fussy palate when it came to textures. I also like to eat things just as they are, without mounds of sugar or processing, so a raspberry is best eaten straight off the plant, still warm, or a tomato, or a fig. Processed sugar is something that you should try to use less of if you can, because it seems to add sweetness at the cost of flavour. Add a little salt or soya sauce to your next raw strawberry – it is weird and rather educational! And replace processed cane or beet sugar with fruit and tree syrups or agave nectar as often as you can. They are wonderful and have flavour that can rival honey, a substance I do miss the taste of.

We have been told by nutritionists for a long time that when you wish to 'detox' your body, you need to simplify your diet, drink lots of water and fruit/vegetables juices and so on. If indeed that is true, then it suggests that things like meat and processed foods are the things toxic to our bodies. So why are we eating them in the first place? Why not abandon them and eat, not a detox diet forever, but a diet that is full of non-toxic foods, and foods that are more energy-efficient: plants.

Plants use very simple ingredients: sunlight, water and carbon dioxide to produce their own foodstuff (sap), their tissues and reproductive parts that develop into fruit or nut bodies, without producing waste or heat. Simple building blocks to make reasonably simple products that still retain much of the energy used to make them. That is energy efficient. They grow quickly and are very adaptable in cooking.

Remember that by plants we are talking about all things pertaining to and coming from plant sources, from roots (carrots, potatoes, beets, etc.), bulbs (onions, garlic, etc.), stems (ginger, leeks, asparagus, etc.), leaves (rocket, cabbage, vines, herbs, etc.), flowers (courgettes, cauliflower, herbs, saffron, broccoli, etc.), seeds, fruits, nuts, cereals, beans, peas and so on. Even the sap of cacti and trees is used for things like maple syrup and oils made from nuts and seeds, syrups from fruits and a plethora of milks, butters, curd and so much more.

Every day I learn of some new process or food that opens up another world of flavour and invention in my kitchen. With all of this plenty and variety, there is everything a human body needs to live a healthy life – bar perhaps Vitamin B12, Iron and, for some, Vitamin D. I take a small supplement (Vitamin B Complex, Vitamin D with Calcium and Iron with Vitamin C) each day, as my intake of these varies depending on the season, the availability in the supermarket and my own appetite. But I have always taken these supplements even as an omnivore. There is an interesting article in *The Vegan* where it states '[…] many non-vegans are B12-deficient, and it is recommended that everyone over the age of 50 should supplement B12' (*The Vegan; The Vegan Magazine*, Autumn 2015, p 5).

Another part of being vegan that I love is the thought of how simple and clean eating plant-based food is. It doesn't involve pain, bodily waste, blood, emotion, stress, animal hormones (plants have their own), injected or ingested antibiotics, steroids, cholesterol (plants have their own that we do not digest), white fat or any of the other rather negative issues surrounding animal-based food. If you buy organic, you can avoid the argument that plants are covered with pesticides and herbicides. There are negatives of course, as there are for anything in life, but they are less intense. Disease is harder to pass on because we are so different from plants, unlike mammals. That is why things such as Mad Cow Disease and Bird Flu are so frightening: they cross the species divide in a way that would never happen with plants and humans. And food poisoning is far more common in meals containing animal products than plant-based ones. There is still the need to be aware of re-heating of things like rice, which can, if done too many times, or after bad storage, lead to high bacteria levels.

You never have to worry about cross-contamination in your kitchen or in your fridge as a vegan, that worry about blood dripping into your lettuces, or blood getting into the cutting board, or cooked and uncooked food getting together. Blood contains innumerable numbers of pathogens, especially poultry and pork juices.

You do, as a vegan, still have to continue to follow hygiene with your food, and keep things in the kitchen clean, your fruit and vegetables washed and fresh.

There are a number of nasty bacterial elements that can grow to toxic proportions if fruit and vegetables are not properly stored and properly washed. And remember that most fruit and vegetables lose their goodness the longer they are stored, so better to buy less and eat it up than bulk shop these items.

If you get as far as growing your own fruit and vegetables, then you reach another level of purity. As long as you stick to organic and biological methods of cultivation (such as encouraging toads in your plot to keep down slugs instead of using slug pellets), you will achieve such a sense of accomplishment, a oneness with your environment and with nature, that it will underpin your vegan beliefs even more firmly. You also learn to share your produce with the wild animals and birds.

We grow figs, blackcurrants, courgettes and greengages (green plums), and would like to grow more but we are rather lazy gardeners. I never kill insects but try to encourage natural answers to things like aphids. I go and collect ladybirds and pop them on-board my aphid-strewn blackcurrants and they do the job of aphid culling the natural way. We do have toads in our veg plot, and over 26 species of bird too, so our insect population is healthy but not overcrowded by any means.

We make our own compost which is full of nutrients and better than using fish blood and bone or other fertilisers. Rotted vegetation is the natural fertiliser, full of nitrogen, essential for plant life.

So get pure, green and downright mucky in the mud if you can. You may only have time and space for a pot of herbs, but do something. It makes so much difference to be in touch with helping to grow something. Unfortunately for us, our three dogs enjoy rampaging through most of what we grow, along with the foxes, but we still make the attempt.

The Protein & Cholesterol Confusion

In one very important nutritional aspect, plants are actually more like animals than you might think. Because they are alive, they contain protein. In fact they are built, grow, and propagate using protein. Every single cell contains protein in its structure and in its functioning parts.

The majority of the general public do not know that fact. And it is no surprise, because we are brought up conditioned in our thinking about food and where our nutrition comes from. As children we are told protein comes from meat, eggs and milk. Remember as a child how you were made to eat an egg, or drink your milk because it would make your bones strong and make you grow healthy?

What was really being said was, having calcium and protein will make your bones strong and make you grow, but the information gets wrapped up in such a way as to get disguised by omnivorous bias. No-one says 'eat those beans because it gives you protein' or 'Here's a handful of nuts for calcium, make your teeth strong'. The only thing you hear is 'Eat your greens' but it often isn't explained why. Even with Popeye to give us a clue to what spinach did to his muscle capacity, no child was told that it was the protein and iron levels of spinach that did the job. Vitamins might get mentioned, but few people know what vitamins are or what they do in the body. If you told a person in the street that the immune system is bolstered by eating mushrooms (due to their Vitamin D) they would probably give you a funny look. Incidentally, the level of Vit D in mushrooms can be pumped up considerably if you place them in the sun, tops upwards, for an hour. Their skins are rather like ours in that they manufacture the vitamin with the use of sunlight, and retain it even when stored or cooked.

The question you will probably hear the most as a vegan is 'How do you know you are getting enough protein?' and I always answer 'Well how do you?' Meat eaters always assume that by eating a lamb chop for dinner they have had their protein for the day.

We are obsessed with protein, and I wonder why, now that I am vegan and understand more about nutrition. As a mother myself, I know only too well how conscious I was about getting milk, cheese and meat down the throats of my young children, so they would grow strong and healthy. Yet I had no education about exactly how much of what to give them. We seem to think that we know. But we don't. Unless it is your job to know.

It is funny, really, that a lot of people are going to quiz you about what you eat, and feel they have some right to tell you what they think about your decision, when it is the non-vegans and non-vegetarians that seem to have the problem when it comes to knowing what and how to eat.

Think about the rise in type 2 diabetes (especially in children), obesity, eating disorders, heart disease, intestinal disorders, weak immunity… The list is endless, not to mention the rise in allergies and food intolerance. And these people eat animal products thinking that it is this food that is natural and right for them, only to be told by their doctor to shift to a vegetarian or vegan diet to control their illnesses.

At least when you decide to be vegan you know that you will need to do some research and think about what you are going to eat. We just don't do that as meat eaters. We just eat what our mothers fed us, and so on. We let social conditioning decide for us without question. It was not our mother's fault, as she followed what she was taught by her own mother, and so on. Little changes happen, such as this recent urge to eat your 'Five a day', which is a very poor intake as it happens. And have we forgotten that the nation was at its healthiest when rationing was imposed during the war? The element of our diet most cut back on, was meat, poultry, eggs and cheese. Well well. There's a surprise.

As for other nutrition, with a little reading you will soon realise that all the things we need are in plants, and we just need to know which ones. As long as you have a varied diet you will probably get everything you need. Amazingly, cholesterol only exists in animal tissue, not in plant, although plants have their own version which is not absorbed by the human intestine (diagnosisdiet.com/food/cholesterol/), so not only do we get protein but we get it cholesterol-free when we eat a plant based diet. Cholesterol is important in every one of our cells, but eating too much ready-made cholesterol isn't so good. Our bodies actually manufacture cholesterol from scratch from various food elements.

I remember reading somewhere a lovely passage about our teeth, and the public belief that we as humans have canines, which means we must therefore eat meat. The passage related our teeth to those of a lion, an obligate carnivore, and to those of a bonobo (ape) that was a forager and fruit eater. It asked the reader to honestly say to themselves whether their own teeth matched the lion's or were in fact more like the bonobos. The piece then went on to say if indeed the reader felt the lion's teeth were a match, to stay the hell away from the writer!

And it isn't just canines. Take a look inside your dog's mouth and at the sides he will have shearing teeth, like secateurs. These are for tearing through muscle tissue and cutting tendons, and molars for crushing bone. Nothing like our teeth at all.

My own personal health has improved since I became a vegan. I have always been pretty healthy, but I have fewer episodes of IBS which has plagued me since my late teens. In fact I haven't even had a sniffle in 24 months as a vegan. My immune system seems stronger, and my energy levels are better. I have lost weight and kept it off. It doesn't see-saw anymore.

It took a year for these changes in my body to settle and become obvious. You can find that at the beginning of your journey you get spots or feel a bit tired as the body detoxes. Give yourself time. Think how long you have been a meat eater. The effect that has had on your mind and body will take time to undo and recalibrate. It is worth the wait and the effort. I hope by now you realise that too.

Where Now

Writing this book has been an absolute pleasure – hard work, frustrating at times as I wanted the recipes to be right, so that when tried by others, the results would be encouraging for them, make them want to continue exploring and trying new things. It meant many meals and desserts I made failed to pass the test. Sometimes they looked good but didn't taste right, or vice versa. It was important to me that each recipe had the crucial elements – colour, texture and taste. It was also crucial that they spark enthusiasm to try things for yourself. Not to be afraid of food and putting it on a plate a little differently to the way you have always been used to. And they had to be family friendly, made in a way that cut out a lot of fuss and bother for busy parents. I do still include more intricate recipes, but overall the food should be very approachable by all, including novice and the experienced.

Getting this section of the book right was important to me too. I didn't want to preach, or be pompous in any way, to judge or force ideas onto anybody. I hope I have got the balance right here, of advice and friendliness, trying to share rather than tell.

This journey into a vegan life, and being able to write about it, has invigorated my own imagination and desire to know more and try more. This is for me, the start of a life of cooking, experimenting and sharing. And writing. Cooking is a craft – it takes practice, but it becomes a passion, an art-form, a lovely way to share your time and love for your family and friends. It has transformed my life and given me a focus I have been seeking for many years. It has also opened my eyes and my heart to many things in this world, and for that I am humbled and encouraged.

Food is a part of what we have sense for. But use the senses you use for other things to come into your kitchen. Think about flavour, colour and shape in a way you see it in nature, the combinations, sometimes perfect and almost designed, sometimes chaotic and sublimely spontaneous. That is your teacher, nature right outside your window.

Nature is also making me wonder about the way we approach veganism. The very word carries with it a preconceived misplaced set of stereotypes, a sense that it is a doctrine or religion that has a code of conduct and laws to follow. It doesn't. In my book, the words vegan and veganism are labels that actually place a millstone around the neck of progress from the meat diet to the plant diet. I would much prefer to have no label, to say I eat food that has roots, a rooted diet. Hence the name of this book. Rooted in compassion, rooted in the future, rooted as the logical, humanitarian and only answer to a future without cruelty, a future that might see an end to starvation too. Rooted to be nourished and stay the course.

Celebrate every day. Help others do the same, not just humans.

I so hope that some of my enthusiasm is transferred to you, and helps you find a clearer and more compassionate path in your life. As a bipolar disorder sufferer, I can truly say that this project, and becoming a vegan has improved my condition and made me realise that new opportunities are always out there waiting, you just have to go look. I might not be able to hold down a full-time job, but I can write a book – a whole one, and hopefully share it with others, so helping them in some way, and helping animals and the environment in the longer term.

I shall continue writing, in fact I am already on my second book. I would love you to accompany me and make our journeys more fun, positive and permanent, transferring what we have discovered to those around us. Take a day at a time, and keep heart, because we are all trying to do our best, and it isn't always easy is it.

There are lots of us now, and times are changing;

> According to a Harris Interactive study commissioned by the Vegetarian Resource Group, approximately five percent of the U.S. is vegetarian (close to 16 million people) and about half of these vegetarians are vegan. While this may sound like a small number, what's amazing is that the number of vegans in the U.S. has doubled since 2009 from 2.5 percent of the population. This means that 7.5 million people in the U.S. now eat diets that do not include any animal products. The study also revealed that 33 percent of Americans are eating vegan/vegetarian meals more often, though they are not vegan or vegetarian.
>
> *August 2015: http://www.onegreenplanet.org/news/is-2014-the-year-of-the-vegan/*

The Vegan Society estimated back in 2006 that there were 150,000 vegans in the UK. They really need to update their sources because it has got to have risen considerably since then, especially when you consider that UK supermarkets are now stocking so many more vegan items and labelling items as vegan for an ever increasingly educated and caring public. Added to this are the dedicated vegan outlets and manufacturers bringing their fayre to our shores:

> This year (2014) will see the German supermarket chain 'Veganz – We Love Life' opening its first branch in the UK, offering over 6,000 vegan products.
>
> *http://www.independent.co.uk/life-style/food-and-drink/features/no-meat-no-dairy-no-problem-is-2014-the-year-vegans-become-mainstream*

Remember this. Change is best done gradually.

Change might seem too small to matter.

But the ocean is after all just a conglomeration of water droplets.

Think big with small steps.

Useful References

My Contacts

Facebook Blog: Fearless Vegan Food Blog

Facebook Page: Fearless Vegan Recipes

Facebook Page: Author Sarah Jay

Twitter: @1FearlessVegan

I am also in a cook book – *Vegan Friends Cookbook* – along with Anja Cass and others. It is available on Blurb.com

Books

I occasionally referred to whilst becoming vegan in my first year;

Sweet by Levi Roots

Prashad by Kaushy Patel

Vegan Indian Cooking by Anupy Singla

Vegan's Daily Companion by Colleen Patrick-Goudreau

The Dal Cookbook by Krishna Dutta

Easy Vegan Cooking by Leah Leneman

Vegan Cooking for One by Leah Leneman

The Joy of Vegan Baking by Colleen Patrick-Goudreau

Magazines

The Vegan Society (via membership)

Vegetarian Living

On-Line Sites for foodstuffs

healthysupplies.co.uk

theveganstore.co.uk

vegantown.co.uk (a specialist for chocolate and sweets)

On-line sites for info

veganvillage.co.uk

veganwolf.com

thevegantruth.blogspot.co.uk

farmanimalrescue.org.uk

everythingpies.com

peta.org

quilnary.com/blog/

happycow.net

http://firstbehealthy.blogspot.co.uk/

http://www.peta.org.uk/issues/animals-not-eat/environment-meat-not-green/

http://evolvecampaigns.org.uk/evolve/default.as

Facebook groups

A few you might find useful to start with – I have found them all to be friendly.

The Vegan Family

Vegan (Supermarket Finds) UK

The Vegan Enthusiast

Vegan

Veggie-Partei

Vegan Friends UK

Plant Strong/Whole Foods

Vegan Food

Earth Friendly Choices

Healthy Foods. We Cook You Eat

Food in Yo Face

Fatass Vegans are Awesome

Create and Share Vegan Project

Veganism

Yummy Vegan Nums

Guilt Free Yum Yum

Meat Free Loveliness

Cruelty Free Info Sites – logos and information

PeTA

PeTA UK

LeapingBunny.org/content/myths-facts

Cruelty Free International (previously BUAV)